**Daddy Doesn't Live Here Anymore**

# Daddy Doesn't Live Here Anymore

### by Rita Turow

**Introduction by Seymour Pastron, M.D.**

GREATLAKES LIVING PRESS
MATTESON, ILLINOIS 60443

**Daddy Doesn't Live Here Anymore**
©Rita Turow 1977
All rights reserved
Printed in U.S.A.
International Standard Book Number: 0-915498-70-7
Library of Congress Catalog Card Number: 77-84660

Greatlakes Living Press Ltd.
21750 Main Street
Matteson, Illinois 60443

# Contents

Acknowledgments
Introduction
Foreword

## WHEN YOU ARE GOING TO DIVORCE   1
1. Telling Your Children   3
2. If Your Child Asks, "Does Your Divorce Make Me Divorced Too?"   8
3. If Your Child Asks, "Is Your Divorce My Fault?"   13
4. "Will You Both Still Love Me?"   19
5. Custody: If Your Child Asks, "Where Will I Live?"   25
6. If Your Child Asks, "Won't I See Daddy (Or Mommy) Anymore?"   31
7. Does It Make a Difference if Your Child Is Adopted?   37
8. If Your Child Asks, "Who Will Take Care of Me Every Day?"   42
9. "What if You Get Sick or Die, Who Will Take Care of Me Then?"   47
10. If Your Child Asks, "Can I Keep My Pet?"   52
11. "If Daddy's Not at Home Will He Still Help Me When I Need Him?"   56

## AFTER THE DIVORCE     63
1. How to Reorganize     65
2. Time Spent With the Parent Who Is Not at Home     71
3. Whose House Does the Child Go to for Holidays?     77
4. What About Your Child and the Grandparents?     83
5. If The Other Parent Says Nasty Things About You to the Child     87
6. Playing One Parent Against the Other     93
7. Lowered Financial Standards     99
8. If It's Your Child's Day With the Other Parent and He Doesn't Show Up     105
9. How Do You Provide Your Child With Adult Companionship if the Other Parent Doesn't Come Around Anymore?     113
10. If You Have to Work     119
11. If Your Child Needs Professional Help     125

## WHEN YOU MARRY AGAIN     131
1. Preparing the Child     133
2. New Stepparents in the House     138
3. Stepbrothers or Sisters     144
4. Worries about Being Disloyal to the Real Mother or Father When You Have a Stepparent     149
5. Worries About Seeing the Real Parent if the Other Parent Remarries     155
6. What Do You Call the New Stepparent?     161
7. Concern About Money for Your Child When You Remarry     165
8. Discipline From the Stepparent     170

**CONCLUSION** 174

**SUGGESTED READING AND OTHER HELPFUL INFORMATION** 175
 1. Related Reading 176
 2. Helpful Agencies 178
 3. Bibliography 191

# ACKNOWLEDGMENTS

My heartfelt gratitude and thanks to Seymour Pastron, M.D., faculty and board member of the Los Angeles Psychoanalytic Society-Institute, who was uncommonly generous of his time and ability and worked with me throughout the preparation of this manuscript.

I am sincerely grateful to the following people who read parts of the material and offered their valuable professional advice:

Martha Kirkpatrick, M.D., Associate Clinical Professor of Psychiatry at the University of California at Los Angeles and current president of the Southern California Psychiatric Society;

Lillian Vittenson, Ph.D., Professor of Clinical Psychology at Northeastern Illinois University;

Calvin Lewis, M.D., Psychiatrist;

Dorothy Kuhl, M.D., Psychiatrist;

Ruth Rubinstein, Family Counselor.

I am most thankful for the wonderful assistance of the following people who gave unstintingly of their special talents:

Fern Brown, author and lecturer whose excellent suggestions inspired the planning of this book;

Isabell Abrams, science and medical writer;

Jane Howard, author and playwright;

Shirley Holab, researcher;

I. Irving Silverman, J.D.;

Jerome Berkson, attorney;

Alvin Becker, D.V.M., who worked with me on the chapter relating to pets;

Ann Dillon, typist and all around Girl Friday.

Thank you to the staff of the Winnetka Public Library, Winnetka, Illinois, who were always so helpful in locating specialized research materials and to the many social service agencies listed at the back of this manuscript who gave me much useful information concerning their activities. Thanks, also to the many agency personnel who spoke with me at length about the problems of children of divorce.

I greatly appreciate the cooperation of the divorced people who were kind enough to answer my surveys and those who permitted me to interview them during the preparation of this work.

My loving thanks to my husband, Dave, who related his experience with patients of divorce in his practice of obstetrics and gynecology and to my writer children, Scott and Vicki, who shared their additional knowledge of law and clinical psychology during the preparation of this manuscript.

While the writer of any book is the prime mover, no work is ever completed without the assistance of many other people. I am deeply grateful for the help I received from all those mentioned in this acknowledgment.

# INTRODUCTION

My uncle died at 76 and my aunt outlived him. They were married for almost 52 years with no separation for more than a few weeks yet they were not particulartly compatible. Every so often, when life's burdens were too much, my aunt would lament, "Oh, if it weren't for the children, I'd get a divorce." The family ignored these complaints. She got over them in a few hours and was busy and contented again. But after my uncle's death I really met my aunt. She emerged. Always a shy person, she became outgoing, and though no entertainer, she reached out to people with a self-assured manner utterly strange to me.

What do we owe each other? I have practiced psychiatry and psychoanalysis for forty years and know no sure answer to that question. Should my aunt have gotten a divorce, paid less attention to the needs of her children for a conventional marriage and let everyone face life with less sheltering from the strain of the unknown? What would have happened? Would my meek, conformist aunt have become a heavy drinking stripper? Would my gruff hard-working uncle have changed his lifestyle and become a devotee of chamber music and poetry? These things are unknowable, but Rita Turow's book describes with deep sympathy and telling insight the cost of divorce to parents and, especially to children. Today the entire world seems in ferment. People seek desperately for the *right* kinds of personal interaction and question more than ever before whether a sedentary conventional life is worth the sacrifice of much of our inner wish to take a chance. They feel more courageous, more willing to disrupt the family for the sake of their own happiness.

Nothing is guaranteed. Many bitter, lonely persons who haven't established new relationships feel divorce is a mistake. Many children look back on a disrupted childhood and deeply regret their parents' separation. But as Rita Turow points out repeatedly, very little is guaranteed in life and there are no correct patterns of behavior which will assure anything to everyone. It's difficult to always separate what is good from what is evil. Greatly ignoring or repressing our selfishness can turn back on itself.

Rita Turow makes two points with which I heartily agree. First, life is always looking for a compromise between individual selfishness and selfless preoccupation with the needs of others. And second, without any universal rules, a loving parent who looks for individual satisfaction as well as the satisfaction of his or her children is more likely to come closer to finding that constantly shifting thread between the contradictory demands of life.

Seymour Pastron, M.D.
Los Angeles, California

# FOREWORD

Divorce was easy in the first century A.D. All you had to do was say "Take your things!" three times in Latin and the union was dissolved. Ending a marriage today is a complex social and legal happening. It is also much more prevalent than at other times in history.

One in three marriages now ends in divorce, most with great trauma and unhappiness to the parties involved. Since the parents are often deeply distressed, it follows that their children must be disturbed as well. They have to make some of the same adjustments as their parents but they usually have a more limited ability to handle the situation. It therefore seems pertinent to explore some of the questions that children of divorce ask and to discuss the answers that could be of help.

The fictional examples in each chapter as well as the anecdotal material are primarily drawn from two sources: a coast-to-coast survey of divorced parents undertaken by the author as well as personal interviews conducted during the writing of this manuscript.

In addition, many of the situations portrayed were described in the course of conferences with highly specialized people in fields relating to the problems of divorce: psychiatrists, psychologists, social workers, family counselors and lawyers.

Whereas the points taken by the incidents that are included remain, the identities of those people mentioned in this book, as well as any of the circumstances that are described, have been completely altered to respect the privacy of the individuals involved.

Other research for this book is noted in the bibliography.

Since nine out of ten mothers gain custody of their children after divorce, the book directs itself more frequently to a mother's problems with children of divorce than it does with the father's. However, the difficulties of divorced fathers who raise their children are also discussed.

The English language makes the handling of pronouns most difficult for a writer. The use of the masculine form where applicable is intended to designate both male and female genders.

This book is designed as a kind of handbook for divorced parents seeking answers to some of the questions most commonly asked by their children.

In all cases where psychological reactions of children are discussed, the reader must understand that the age of every child and his background will alter his responses.

The information here is offered as a general guide and is not intended as a substitute for professional help that should be obtained if problems persist.

Rita P. Turow
Winnetka, Illinois
Summer 1977

*To Dave, my husband,
who offers me every
kind of support
and to my mother who
taught me to appreciate
the written word*

# PART I

# WHEN YOU ARE GOING TO DIVORCE

# Part 1 Chapter 1

# Telling Your Children

Divorce tolls the death of a marriage and is difficult to explain to children. When parents decide that separation is inevitable they must deal with the questions that terrify most children. Why are Mommy and Daddy going to divorce? What will happen to me? Do they still love me? The parents must answer in a way that is truthful yet permits some feelings of security to remain with their children who are threatened by the shattering end of the parents' marriage.

* * * * * *

It had finally come to this, Millie thought. This was the day she and Jim had decided to tell their children about the impending divorce. Their resolve to end all the arguments, bickering and bad feelings produced a kind of sterile calm that even the children seemed to sense. Howard, aged 7, 9-year-old Chuckie and Carrie, their 4-year-old daughter, talked softly in the blue tiled breakfast room as they finished their cereal and milk.

It was time. Millie nodded toward their father. He paled, pushed his empty coffee cup aside and cleared his throat.

"Kids," he began, "your mother and I want to talk to you."

Millie's mouth felt dry. "There is something that we need to tell you," she added reaching for a water glass.

Innocent, the children looked to their parents.

"Kids," Jim started again. "Your mother and I have been unhappy for quite awhile now."

Howard looked worried. "Oh, it has nothing to do with you kids at all," their father reassured them. "It's not anything you have done. It's about us, your mother and me." He cracked the knuckles on his hands. "When we married, we really loved each other and thought we would live together forever — but now that's not possible." His voice trailed off and he looked toward Millie who continued for him.

"Daddy and I have been so unhappy with each other that we each want to live in different houses from now on." She paused hoping she was striking the right tone. "We know this is upsetting for you. It is for us, too, but we hope it will be better for all of us after we separate." She took a deep breath. "So, what we want to tell you is that Daddy and I are going to get a divorce."

There was an unnatural silence. The children's faces looked blank for a moment, then frightened.

Howard was the first to react. "What will happen to us? Where will we go?"

Jim replied quickly. "You'll be here with your Mom, same as always and you'll come and see me very often in my new apartment. Your grandmother Benson will live here with you and Mommy, too. We'll tell you all about the arrangements later on."

Carrie looked from one parent to the other. "What's a divorce?" she asked, puzzled.

Millie placed her small daughter on her lap. "That's what you call it, when people end a marriage." Then she turned to her sons. "Daddy and I will try to answer all your questions after you think about what we've told you."

Chuckie was the last to speak. He sounded confused and unhappy. "Do you still love us?"

Jim hugged his two sons. "Of course we love you. We'll never stop loving the three of you and we'll always take care of you."

Millie was on the verge of tears. "Darlings, darlings, you'll always have us." She was too choked up to continue.

All three looked so miserable—so vulnerable. And they, the parents, had done this to their own children.

It's done, Millie thought. We'll have to tell each one over and over again that we love them. But they'll have to bear the pain alone. She prayed inwardly. I hope we all have better days ahead.

\* \* \* \* \* \*

Most everyone who contemplates the dissolution of his marriage goes through periods of indecision. Should we stay together for the sake of the children? Will it work out after all? Children should not be told of the possibility of divorce until the wavering is over and the parents are certain that their marriage is at an end.

When the pain of staying together is so intense that a mother and father arrive at a firm agreement to divorce, they should set a time to discuss it with the children and tell them of their decision.

Both parents should tell the children together. Having the mother and father present makes for more evenhanded telling and prevents the possibility of the children having to take sides. If there is more than one child in a family they should all be told at one time. The presence of brothers and sisters offers an emotional buttress against such devastating news.

Most parents feel guilty about the chaos they are about to bring to their children. They know that the kids will suffer because of their decision.

A San Francisco father who was against telling the children about the divorce in the family admitted that he couldn't stand the idea of inflicting pain on his children. "I could just see the fright and fear on my children's faces and it broke me up just thinking about it," he said. "It took me more than a week to work up the courage to tell them."

At such a time parents are not readily able to accept that children may eventually be better off in a happy single-parent home than they were in a two-parent home disturbed by constant anger.

It's tempting for some to avoid telling children of an oncoming divorce knowing that all family members are usually aware of dissension in the home. Nevertheless, it is better to tell kids than to let them guess. Parents must let children know what will happen to them. If the mother or father are planning a move or if the children's home will be elsewhere they should be told so that they can begin to make an adjustment. It's shocking to have a parent just disappear from home without prior explanation. Telling your child makes eventual acceptance of the change in his life easier to bear.

One parent suggested that she failed to tell her child about her divorce because she didn't know how or what to say. "I didn't know how to tell my 5-year-old son that his father and I were calling it quits," she explained. "At first everything seemed all right and my son was content. Then one day he exploded with rage. He was screaming, kicking, biting and crying all at once. Fortunately it was his father's visiting day, and he arrived in time to help quiet the boy."

Later, outside counseling was needed to help the child get

over his emotional reactions.

When exactly should you tell your children you've decided to terminate your marriage? Should you tell them long before the actual divorce takes place? This is a matter of personal judgement. It prolongs the agony to inform a child too far in advance of a divorce. On the other hand, preparing your children before the occurrence, while both parents are still under the same roof, may help the child work through his reactions and become accustomed to the idea. Children need to be told of future family arrangements with tact and consideration.

Many psychiatrists feel *how* you tell your children about your impending divorce is almost more important than *what* you are saying. Be calm. Decide ahead of time what you are going to say. It will make it easier to explain. Try to be affirmative, but don't be too hard on yourself if you become emotional in discussing the change that will soon take place. It's not necessary to pretend that you feel none of the confusion and unhappiness your children are feeling. If you can, however, avoid hysteria when you are telling your children about your impending divorce. It will be much easier for your kids. Parents are the model for their children's behavior. If your children see that you are saddened, but calm, and are going to try to work out the problems, it offers them incentive to do the same.

How much should you tell your children about your marital discord? As mentioned earlier, they are often already aware of some of the problems. Try to be as honest as possible without overburdening them with details which are beyond their ability to comprehend. Explain briefly extreme situations such as illness, drug addiction or alcoholism. Painful as it may be for a parent to describe, it is better for the children to have some knowledge from the home than to have a neighbor's child inform them about the difficulties in his house.

One parent should not blame the other or make it seem that one is "the good one" and the other is "the bad one." Emphasize that it is better for both parents to live apart. Tell your children that they will not be abandoned and that your love for them will continue.

All children must be reassured from the onset of any discussions that they had absolutely nothing to do with your decision to divorce and that the problem exists between the mother and father only. Even if your child has heard you arguing about him, tell him that it points up your inability to agree about anything.

When you tell your children about your divorce, make certain to include all family members in the discussion. Even very young children will understand something of the problem if they are present.

Reassure your children of your continuing love and care. Tell them over and over again. Let them learn the lesson by rote hearing, as they would learn the mathematical tables of two's and three's. Be sure to reinforce your words with loving behavior.

Under most circumstances, explanations to your children will be difficult. In the interest of their emotional stability, don't delay too long. Tell your children what to expect so they can work through the adjustment and get on with their lives.

## Part 1 Chapter 2
## If Your Child Asks, "Does Your Divorce Mean That I'm Divorced Too?"

One of the fears that many children have after the disruption of their parent's marriage is that they too have been divorced from either the mother or father who no longer lives at home. There is a justifiable concern that even if the absent parent arranges to see a child often, the continuity of shared living experiences will no longer exist and he will feel truly separated from that parent.

* * * * * *

A month after Helen told her 5-year-old daughter about her decision to divorce, she overheard Patty at play.

"You're a bad girl," Patty said to her doll, removing her from the doll house that sat in the corner of her bedroom floor. The child flung her blond curls aside. "I'm going to divorce you!"

Sharon, her 4-year-old friend sat beside her. "What's a divorce?" she asked in her baby voice.

Patty spanked the doll as she answered. "That's when someone goes away from your house. That's what divorce is."

"My brother goes away. He goes to school," said Sharon.

Patty shook her head. "No, not like that. It's for daddies." Then her voice assumed a sing-song. "They go away-away and they never come back," and after a pause she added, "except once in a while." Patty spanked the doll again and again and shook her to make her cry.

Sharon watched Patty. "Tommy's mother went away," she said. "She's a divorce too."

A few weeks later Helen overheard the children once again. This time they were watching a television show in which one of the characters had disappeared. "He's gone. He's a divorce." Patty ducked her blond curly head under a throw pillow on the couch. "Now I'm a divorce." She giggled in a muffled voice.

"I want a turn to be a divorce." Sharon tried to grab the pillow away.

"You can't be a divorce. Your daddy comes home. My mommy and I are divorced because our daddy is gone."

Sharon stamped her foot. "I want to be divorced too."

Patty was adamant. "You can't be. Only my mommy and me. We're divorced." She dodged Sharon's advance on the pillow.

Sharon dissolved into tears. "I'll tell my mommy on you. I'll tell my mommy you said you're a divorce and I'm not." She paused for a moment. "I'll tell my daddy on you too." Then with new thought she turned back and taunted Patty. "You haven't got a daddy anymore." She stuck her tongue out at Patty. Now satisfied that she had somehow evened up the score, she bounced out of the house.

It was Patty's turn to cry. Helen tried to comfort the child. "Why did Daddy divorce us?" Patty sobbed.

"But he didn't," Helen reassured her. "Only he and I were divorced. It had nothing to do with you."

Patty shook her head and wailed. "No, no. He doesn't love me anymore. He doesn't come to see me. I'm a divorce too." She screamed her reply.

Helen was disturbed. She telephoned her ex-husband. He agreed that they should both try to convince their daughter that their divorce had nothing to do with her. If that didn't help, they would have to talk to someone else. They couldn't let their daughter go on thinking she was also divorced.

Or was she? Perhaps the child was right after all. The legalities didn't define her as such, but wasn't she in effect deprived of the other parent as though she were divorced too? It wasn't just the decree. It was the fact that they were now living separate lives.

• • • • • •

Children feel pitifully alone after a divorce and need the stability and support of parents. It's a highly painful loss for all family members and is ranked by psychiatrists as the most powerful loss next to death. The structure of each individual family has a certain physical make-up. There is a mother, a father and the children. Now suddenly this structure is altered by divorce and there is a void. One of the two most important members is gone and the former physical shape of the family is destroyed. Without adequate reassurance, the child feels separated, divorced and bereft of one parent.

If parents handle divorce and separation well, it is far easier for children to accept parental absence from the home. Children usually reflect the attitudes of the remaining parent. If a mother or father accepts the new role as a single parent and goes about the business of settling into a routine in a one-parent home in a positive manner, the child will follow the lead and adjust.

During the adjustment, if a parent feels great unhappiness at the absence of the other parent, it is better to include the children and let them mourn too. It is important not to shut your children out. If you do, they may feel they have not only lost one parent but also the other, who is grief-stricken, and unwilling or unable to share his feelings with the remaining members of the family.

Such reluctance sets a poor example for encouraging your children to discuss their problems concerning the parent who no longer lives at home. Children should always be encouraged to express themselves. Getting feelings into the open is one way of avoiding anxiety build-up that bubbles around inside you. "Talking it out" has a discharging quality and often relieves emotional pressure.

Some parents encourage children to talk to them by having rap sessions where they may say anything, even to the point of being highly critical, so that a relationship can be developed where both can communicate.

One father in Oklahoma, hearing of these open rap sessions, commented, "We don't need to encourage kids to be critical. Whose kids aren't these days? When I was growing up we never spoke to our parents the way they do today."

But most parents agree that being able to discuss things openly is an excellent idea. The child needs to talk about their real concerns and parents need to listen with honesty and interest.

Much as mothers and fathers would like to feel otherwise, divorce is as difficult for children as it is for the parents. Children who feel strongly that they are also divorced by the legalities are sometimes a long time getting over it.

Cally, now a New York matron, was a tiny child when her mother and father separated. At the time of her own marriage, she recalled her feelings about her parents' divorce. When her father moved to another state, her mother took a full-time job. She and Cally then went to live with a loving aunt and uncle.

# DADDY DOESN'T LIVE HERE ANYMORE

On the eve of Cally's own marriage, her real father, uninvited, arrived at the wedding rehearsal. Cally was closeted with him for the better part of an hour, after which he left and she never heard from him again.

"Why did you send him away?" her uncle later asked. "He is your father." Though it had been years ago, her anger was still remembered. "I didn't want him around," she declared. "Just because he divorced my mother, it didn't mean he had to divorce me too."

One has only to watch children alone in situations where the needed parent is absent to know why many children feel that they were also divorced. There are hundreds of school occasions when the child from a one-parent home must suffer singly and watch other children enjoying the support and comfort of a loving father or mother. Sometimes children may avoid such occasions and spare themselves the heartache of having to face up to an activity alone. An endless parade of outings, theatrical performances, school exercises or even birthdays are lost to the child with one absent parent and one harried working parent who can't afford to take off from work for such seeming frivolities.

Often a hospitalized child may be terrified by the lack of a supportive parent to help him through an illness. Sometimes, too, frightened children must bear the illness of the remaining parent alone.

In a way divorce can be harder to accept than death. The termination of life can be laid to a higher force. From birth on, every person knows that he or she will die. There is no one to blame and no way to remain immortal. But loss of a parent through a wholly legal set-up, leaves many reasons for remorse, anger, fear and limitless aloneness.

Another problem for the child who feels she or he has been divorced along with the parents is the compact structure of the modern family. No longer do we live in large family units that include grandparents, many brothers and sisters and perhaps a spare unmarried aunt or uncle. Early in the history of the United States any toppling of the pinnacle member in the family structure was buffered by the presence of many remaining relatives. It is true that the heads of families were almost always lost through death. However, the loss of a mother or father did not upset the family organization.

Today with smaller families, the relationship between parents and children is necessarily concentrated in a much smaller group so that the loss of one member through divorce affects all of the few remaining members. There are no longer assorted relatives to cushion the blow.

Divorce has become such a common social condition that one happily married Eastern saleswoman related that her eight-year-old son expressed his rage at his older brother by stating, "I'm mad at you. I'm going to divorce you."

His mother explained that children weren't involved in divorce.

But he countered, "Yes they are. Look at Jeremy." He named his friend next door. "He and his dad are divorced from his mother."

In a situation where a child feels he or she has in effect been divorced from one parent, reassurance is extremely necessary. It is important to tell the child over and over again that the divorce had nothing to do with him and that he is not involved in the divorce. The child must know that the condition of being a child is not changeable and that no matter what happens with the mother and father, he or she is still their child. It is an irrevocable contract and remains, despite the rupture between the parents. Tell your child that your marriage may have failed but that having your child was the happiest part of your marriage for both of you. It is important to restate your feelings of caring and love for your child.

Even though one parent may be absent much of the time, the time together can be very important if the visiting parent will behave with understanding and love. Responsible parents will try to do what is best for the children.

It is paramount importance for the child not to feel that he has been abandoned as a result of the divorce and that he, through no fault of his own, has lost a parent as though death were the cause.

When one considers the numbers of parents who want only to lose interest in children after a divorce or fail to show any real interest following a failed marriage, it is no wonder that some children may feel they were divorced too. The wonder is that more children do not feel this way.

The advisable thing to do is to explain and repeat and repeat. Repetition is a learning process. Try to talk it out with your child so that eventually he will understand that he was not divorced in the courtroom when you were.

## Part 1 Chapter 3

## If Your Child Asks, "Is Your Divorce My Fault?"

**Children sometimes suspect that they have been the unwitting cause of parental separation. Young children, especially, may worry that their anger or bad thoughts were so powerful that they caused the family to come apart. When children feel responsible for a mother and father's divorce, they are guilt ridden and blame themselves for what has happened.**

\* \* \* \* \* \*

Nancy felt tense and unhappy as she cleared away the children's dishes. "This is the last day of this part of my life!" she said aloud. She and Richard had agreed that tonight they would gather the children and tell them of their plans to divorce.

As if to tidy up the last bits and pieces of her life with Richard, she straightened the kitchen counters and filled a bucket with hot soapy water. Then she carefully mopped the entire yellow surface. Finishing with a degree of satisfaction she surveyed the clean room.

Suddenly Buddy, her young son, burst through the back door. His heavy football shoes were layered with oozing mud, and he dragged a dirt-filled football helmet into the kitchen.

"Look Mom!" He was choked with laughter. "Tony threw me into the mud. But you should see what I did to him!"

Nancy felt her stomach muscles tighten. Her shining floor showed a trail of mud and footprints. She exploded! "Is this your idea of fun? Look at my floor!" she screamed. "You're 10 years old! It's time you started to think of *me* once in awhile." Richard, having just arrived home, strode into the room. He scowled. "Just another friendly mother and son chat?" His words dripped with sarcasm. "Up to your usual rotten tricks, I see." He addressed his son.

And the fight was on!

Buddy looked so unhappy. "I'm sorry," he mumbled backing up towards the door. As he listened to the rising argument between his mother and his father he felt more and more guilty. His thoughts made him feel even worse. Why did I come into the house with all that mud? It's me. I'm always making them fight. They're always fighting about something I did!

In days to follow Buddy mentioned this scene and others like it to his mother. "I guess it's my fault you and dad are getting a divorce." He was miserable. "I'm always doing stuff like that and causing trouble."

"It's not your fault at all," his mother consoled him. "Dad and I have a problem with each other. It would have been a good idea to have left your muddy shoes and dirty football helmet outside before you came into the house, but that isn't what's causing our divorce. We are just not happy with each other. You are not to blame." She hugged the worried boy.

It was a good conversation for Buddy.

* * * * * *

Frequently children will feel their bad behavior is a cause of their parents' separation, so it's important to make them understand something of their parents' divorce. They must be told that the parents are getting divorced because they are unhappy with one another, and can no longer live in the same house. It is *not* because the children have been bad.

Divorce is a traumatic time in one's life and it is difficult to think of a child as another person who is also trying to cope with the effects of the problems without the necessary defenses and maturity. Children may sense tension in the household or hear violent arguments. They can understand that they are sometimes the focal point of eruptions between a mother and father. Often a parent feels so unhappy that he or she takes his own misery out on the child.

In the face of increased bad feelings, sometimes involving the child, a decision to divorce may make your child feel he is at fault.

Very young children sometimes have problems understanding that thoughts and action are not the same thing. If such a child wishes that a punitive father would leave him alone and the father then moves out, he may be certain his thoughts caused the divorce to happen.

Children must be reassured that their inner rage does not make things happen. Regardless of age, any guilty child should be assured that a parent's anger at their misdeeds does not cause divorce either.

There are no exact formulas for human behavior so one can only work out the puzzle of unhappy relationships with spoken words and gestures in hopes of increasing good feeling.

"I felt so much better after Mom and Dad talked to me a couple of times and said I wasn't to blame for their divorce," said Sandra, a Chicago high school student. "I thought at first it happened because of me. I never came right home after school and there were always fights at supper. Mom said I was a wanderer like Dad, or Dad would tell Mom she couldn't even control me. When they got their divorce, I felt so guilty at first and then it was such a relief to know it wasn't really my fault."

Authorities agree that it is important to tell a child that a family break-up is not his fault. Dr. Seymour Pastron, a Los Angeles psychoanalyst, suggests that at the first announcement of a divorce, children must be assured that the parents' problem alone is the cause and that divorce was not caused by the children.

When children feel responsible for their parents' divorce they will read meaning into subsequent conditions. One mother went back to work full time following divorce and sent her child to a day care center. The child, already feeling he was the cause of what happened, now felt that he was being put out of the house every morning as a punishment for his bad behavior and that, furthermore, his mother didn't really want him all the time and was taking this way of getting rid of him. Each morning there was a small upset and minor revolution trying to pack the child off to the center. When the child developed measles shortly thereafter the mother realized how much happier the child was to remain at home. After he recovered, his grandmother came to stay with him until he had made a better adjustment to having his mother gone.

In general, following such traumatic household disruption as divorce, it is best to stay with the existing pattern of living if at all possible.

If a parent is going to move, it is best not to do it immediately. It is difficult enough to have had one parent leave the house. A guilty child may feel that moving is another form of punishment visited upon him for being the causative factor in a family split. It is usually easier to make the transition if the rest of a child's life goes on at a familiar pace and he is comforted by his toys, his friends or even the same neighbor next door.

If the mother or father must move, they should try to stay in the same area. One west coast woman attorney looked for a house just a few blocks away from his father, who still lived in their old house.

Of course, divorce frequently means the loss of real contact with one parent. Once the relationship is severed many parents drift away and after a few feeble attempts at visiting their offspring, go off and make a new life for themselves that does not include any members of their former families.

In that case the children must be made to understand that they had no part in the loss of contact with the parent and that they were not to blame for what transpired. They too should then be encouraged to make a new life for themselves without the parent who has left them.

It's important that a child should not feel that the loss of contact with a parent is a form of punishment because he's *bad* or that he, the child, is somehow being *paid back* because he caused the divorce.

"Tell them, tell them endlessly that they are not at fault for the parents' divorce," advises Dr. Seymour Pastron.

One parent complained that her child started to wet his bed following her divorce. Usually, but not always, bed-wetting is an expression of anxiety and insecurity. Generally anxious or insecure children wet their beds when they recall the stage of life when wetting was permissible and accepted. They recall being a baby with pleasure and seek to imitate that time.

However annoying such regressive behavior may be for the parent, try not to scold and don't shame your child. He is not trying to be naughty. Don't chastise him with any form of punishment. Do try to remain calm about it so that your anxiety-ridden child will not become even more anxious. Help your child get up at night to go to the bathroom. Keep a little light on so that if he gets up and wants to get out of bed he can see his way there alone.

If some measure of bladder control is achieved, offer praise, but not in such a way that it will appear as loss of approval the nights he doesn't make it. Perhaps you can say, "Maybe tomorrow will be a dry night again. We'll see." If he's receptive to the idea you might even try having some kind of check chart when the child has had a dry night. Whatever you do, don't make an issue of his problem.

Family counselor Ruth Rubinstein suggests children have complex reasons for lack of toilet training, whether they are angry or gratified on the one hand or feel helplessly gripped by something beyond their control. "Should their bed wetting be tied in with divorce and its problems," says Miss Rubinstein, "professional help may be needed to unite the melange of anger, self-righteousness, guilt and fear."

There are frequent reactions to divorce. It would be unusual not to have any at all. Suddenly a child's life changes in a very dramatic way. His world is torn apart and the total makeup is altered. It isn't children alone who react to such change. It affects everyone who undergoes such an experience. It is a most human response.

It's extremely difficult for those children who have to witness courtroom battles relating to their parents' marital woes. A child must feel terribly guilty listening to an airing of personal disputes between two of the most important people in his life.

Some communities, aware of these disruptive forces, are attempting to provide alternatives for the children whose parents are thus occupied. A private group in the city of Chicago has set up a play room situation as a day care center near the divorce court room. Children can play or nap without being subjected to the divisive battles ensuing nearby.

If your child is able to talk about his upset over your divorce, encourage him to express himself. Do try to show a sincere interest in his problems. Listen to him. Be loving and kind. Try to answer any of the questions he may want to ask and don't give any phoney answers. Children are quick to ferret out insincerity. Don't put him off with "You're too young to understand." Try to answer with honesty. If your child asks why you had so many arguments, say you're not sure but that you did not seem to be able to agree on most things and that it made you both unhappy. Again emphasize that your dissension did not include your child and that he did not cause the problem between you. Be gentle but don't be wishy-washy. Be firm and offer your child the security of knowing that the situation will not change even though it is not anyone's fault.

With time your child will usually develop secure relationships with the one remaining parent or with both of the separated parents. A secure child is less inclined to feel a divorce was his fault.

If ever your child shows signs of thinking he was to blame for your rift, assure him that he was not. Say it. Say it with a hug and a kiss. Reassure him often. Let him know you really mean it when you say there were grown-up problems between his mother and father and that he had nothing to do with it.

A happier child will make your life happier too.

# Part 1 Chapter 4
# "Will You Both Still Love Me?"

**Learning about the changes that divorce is bringing, a child may fear that every facet of his life will be altered. Parental love is of such major importance that the child may worry that his mother and father will no longer love him once the separation has been accomplished. Since the parents no longer love each other, he may reason that the withdrawal of love also extends to him.**

* * * * * *

Katie seemed entranced by the puppet show on the television screen. Her mother's voice floated out from the kitchen. "Time to eat," the voice said. But the puppets were dancing and tossing colored balloons that were stamped with the word LOVE. Katie sighed as she heard the voice from the kitchen call again. This time it sounded louder. Suddenly Katie's mother burst into the room. She towered over the little girl seated on the floor and grabbed her by the arm. "Damn it!" she screamed, pulling the little girl into the kitchen. "Do I have to call you and call you whenever it's time to eat? I've got enough to do around here without you making it harder and harder for me."

Katie erupted into tears. Ever since her daddy went away everything seemed wrong. Her mother was always angry with her and yesterday when she was with her father he seemed anxious to get rid of her. He had brought her home earlier than usual and he hadn't taken her to the movie as he had promised the week before.

"Now, don't cry Katie," he said as he brought her into the apartment. "I have to catch an early plane for my appointment. I'll make it up to you." He quickly kissed the top of her head.

"By the way, I'll be out of town for a few weeks, so I won't be by for Katie," he said to her mother, who had opened the door for them.

Katie's mother was angry. "Well, what am I supposed to do? I've got plans for the next two Sundays. I won't be around, so why don't *you* figure out what to do with her." Katie was frightened. They don't love me anymore, she said to

19

herself. No one wants me. They used to love me but they don't anymore.

Shortly after that Katie developed a twitch in her face. She seemed always to be working her mouth in peculiar circles. She complained of stomach aches and frequent urination.

"I don't know what's gotten into her," Katie's mother explained to their pediatrician. "She's always making the most awful faces. I'm the one who could be making faces. I've had a really hard time since Ron and I divorced."

But Katie was the one who was going to have an even harder time as a result of her parents' divorce. Her mother appeared to be totally involved with her own adjustment to her different lifestyle and felt encumbered by her child.

Ron, Katie's father, was involved with his job, and his attention to Katie was a secondary thing. Small wonder that Katie felt unloved.

* * * * * *

Love is to human development what sunshine is to a growing plant. It's a real necessity. Everyone basks in the warm glow of love and grows with security and grace. Without it, emotional development is stunted and confined.

From infancy on the small child derives a sense of security from the nourishment and warmth and love provided by its mother. Every tiny child responds to being cuddled. A mother's smile and cooing words please an infant. A crying baby finds it is comforting to be held and loved.

A growing child will try to give his or her love to the mother or father as well as receive it. Children like to offer parents a loving token. Perhaps they will craft a wad of clay or use crayons to scratch a picture. Most of us have experienced the shapeless marks of a small child who has concentrated over some piece of paper and then lovingly gifted it to the mother, father or some other favorite person, such as a grandparent. The wavering angular marks are unidentifiable but nevertheless represent sheer, unadulterated love in every irregular scrawl.

At first a child's world centers on mama but as he begins to be more aware of his surroundings he crawls and then walks in exploration until he is able to turn his total concentration away from his mother and begins to develop an attachment for his father.

"Adrienne was almost glued to me at first. She wanted to

be near me all the time until she started to walk and only then, it seemed, she discovered her father," a young Chicago mother explained.

In the very earliest stages of life, daddy is not as important as mommy, but a little later on he may be the parent who shows the child the glittering facets of living. For instance, it may be father who takes the child to the amusement park or baits his or her line in the first attempt at fishing. Perhaps it is the father who guides tiny roller skates on the new skater or shows the way to maneuver the wheels on a new bike.

Father usually lays down the ground rules in the household. His words are law. He also offers guidance and love. Daddy is a kind of teacher who can help the child work out some of his or her problems and serves as a model for the child's view of the male figure, just as mother is the example for the female figure. Children grow in the loving watchfulness of parents until they mature and eventually become the mother and father of others in the endless process of reproduction and growth.

What happens to the child who feels unloved? What about the child caught in the vise of bad behavior of two parents who are bruised by their divorce and who are so consumed by their own hurt that they either resent the child or pay little attention to him or her?

The child who feels deprived of love, for whatever reason, will be very insecure. A child of divorce, feeling unloved, may also feel a sense of personal worthlessness. They do not feel that they merit being loved. Dr. Seymour Pastron explains, "A child may feel that the evil within him or her may have caused the parents to divorce and, therefore, he or she is responsible for what is happening." If one is bad, such reasoning extends, why should anyone bother loving him?

How to explain love? It has an ephemeral quality. You can't hold it, yet you can feel it. You can't taste it but it adds spice to your life. It is one of the most important feelings to a whole human being. It accounts for a sense of well being and happiness. A person can be loved himself or give his or her love to another and be a loving being. It is the giving and taking of love in a family that creates good relationships between parents and children. It goes hand in hand with accepting attitudes about family members and genuine caring of one for the other. A child of divorce needs to feel that he still has the love of each parent and that they still care about him.

"Glenn took our divorce in stride," an Arizona father explained, "but his mother and I spent a lot of time letting him know we loved him and that our love for him was not going to be withdrawn because we were living in two separate houses."

A child learns love first from the mother who helps, protects and nourishes her offspring. A small child is a defenseless being who is totally dependent upon his mother. A mother's freely given care and concern for the baby teaches him how to offer love. Even when children reach a point where they no longer need to lean on the parents, a loving mother and father will delight in their development. Security permits them to separate from the mother and father and grow independently. Our behavior toward our children is a blueprint for their behavior toward us and toward others.

In the same way, children must have a good regard for themselves that grows out of the good regard shown them by their parents. The love and security a child gains in infancy serves as a guide for his responses to others throughout his entire life.

Withholding love so that a child feels disapproval can lead to anxiety, guilt and endless complications. Most of us are not happy to feel a momentary loss of love when someone shows that they disapprove of our behavior. A child feels even more unhappy when a mother disapproves of him.

Throughout our lives our behavior toward other people will reflect the emotional behavior we learned by interacting with our parents. It is, therefore, very important to a child's well being that he grows up feeling loved and accepted. It cannot be said often enough. When someone cares about us, we are able to pass it on and care about someone else. What we learn as children influences our adult behavior and our later reactions to our own children. It goes on and on like the life cycle itself. Each generation passes something of its emotional pattern on to the next one coming up.

"I still remember how I felt when I was seven," an old college chum once confided. "My parents did not get along and were always bickering. I recall one Mother's Day when Dad actually remembered Mom with an orchid silk scarf and large box of candy. For a change there were pleasant words between them. I still remember how surprised Mom was and how pleased she looked. It made me so happy! I recall watching them intensely and savoring each happy moment. Last year Harry brought me a scarf and a box of candy when he returned from a business trip. Suddenly, I remembered that incident when I was seven, and do you know, I enjoyed that gift more than the gold pin he gave me for my following birthday."

Observe yourself inching your car along on a busy street, pushing forward and trying to break into another lane of traffic. Someone lets you get ahead of him. Suddenly, you are more considerate and polite to another driver who must break in ahead of you. The feeling is contagious; like love.

Loving behavior inspires loving behavior!

If your child asks if you will both still love him when you are getting a divorce, say *yes*. Tell your child that you will coninue to feel the same love towards him. Even if your child doesn't ask the question aloud he may be thinking it. A little reassurance goes a long way. Say that you will always feel love for your child whether or not you continue to live in the same house. Explain that mother has her work in the house and perhaps a job, and that dad has his work, most likely away from the house but that your child is very important to both of you and that you will see your son or daughter whenever you can.

Try to spend time with your children. Try to help them when they're troubled as an extension of your love.

A recently divorced mother related the following anecdote. "Terry's teacher seemed to make a big thing out of needing room mothers. Terry felt self-conscious because it seemed to her that everyone's mom had done something for the room except hers. I was working," Terry's mother explained, "so I couldn't come to the classroom and help with some of the chores in the room, but I sent a note to school offering to wash the room curtains. You should have seen how happy Terry was when her teacher complimented the freshly laundered curtains!"

"Mom, Miss Kinley said the curtains looked just beautiful," Terry was beaming. Then she reached over and squeezed her mother. "I love you, Mom."

Terry's mom had shown that she loved Terry, too, by recognizing her discomfort at not having her mother participate in the room mother's program, and trying to do something within the framework of the time she had to offer.

Comfort your child and stand by him when illness strikes. Think how good love and kindness makes you feel when you're sick, and translate this feeling to your children.

Show your child that you love him by going out of your way to look pleased or to be helpful. This may be a tall order to a parent who is still hurt or angry about a recent divorce, but if you want your child to really feel that you are paying more than lip service, you need to stretch your efforts a little.

It's entirely possible that in your own unsettled state you may think to yourself, "Why do I have to put myself out, especially when I feel so lousy? Why me? Let the child put himself out for me for once in a while. Or better still, let the other parent do it. I'm always the one."

You can't be responsible for the other parent's conduct toward your child, but you do know what you are doing and saying. You've already learned a pattern of behavior from *your* parents. Now whatever you do sets the example of emotional well being for your child.

No matter how difficult it seems at the moment, one of the nicest benefits is that it will all come back to you later like a lovely bonus. You give love and your child will return it to you. They learn how to be loving from you.

## Part 1  Chapter 5

## Custody:
## If Your Child Asks,
## "Where Will I Live?"

Many couples enter into negotiations for divorce without realizing how upsetting the prospect is for children, worried about their own security. Before custody is decided, a child may feel his entire world has been shattered. Even after making a decision concerning his future the child may feel uncomfortable knowing that this new arrangement will lack one of the parents most of the time.

* * * * * *

"I wanna piece of pizza, too." Dottie put her toy down and reached out to her brother, who was trying to work some of the oozing cheese pie off of the round cardboard.

"Wait a minute," he admonished her. "Miralee is first. She gets the first piece." He slid a sticky mass onto a small paper plate and handed it to his middle sister.

"Mamma said I could have some pizza first. I wanna piece now," Dottie whined.

Kenny, her 12-year-old brother, turned on her. "Darn you Dottie," he glowered. "You're the worst 7-year-old! You're a regular pain in the neck. Mamma spoiled you rotten. Wait till it's your turn, will you?" He returned to the layered mass of cheese and sausage.

Nine-year-old Miralee took a bite of her pizza. "Ummm delicious!" She passed the plate under Dottie's nose and withdrew it out of her sister's reach.

"Miralee's teasing me. Kenny, she's teasing me," Dottie cried out as she threw her toy at her sister. It missed but managed to hit the corner of the large pizza and knock it on the kitchen floor.

The next second after this declaration of war all three children were yelling, fighting, twisting and crying.

Mrs. Jefferson, the landlady, came running up the back stairs. "What's going on here," she shouted. "Can't you kids keep still until the end of my program?" Then seeing the mess, "Oh, my God. You'd think with your mamma and daddy having so much trouble with the divorce and fighting about you kids that you'd all know enough to behave." As she knelt to clean up the mess on the kitchen floor her anger increased. "I should think you kids would be too worried about where you're going to live now that your mother and father are both getting married to someone else. You keep this up, and no one is going to want you." She shook the damp towel at them. "No one wants a bunch as messy as you three," she reiterated.

The children stopped fighting. They looked frightened. "Who said they won't want us?" Kenny was trying to sound brave.

"Ya, Uncle Don likes us. He said so." Miralee stuck her tongue out at Mrs. Jefferson.

"Don't you stick your tongue out at me," the large woman shook her. "Now you kids behave. I'm sick of all of you, with your mama's Uncle Don and your dad's friend Celine." She shook her head. "And all the rest of that hippie bunch that comes in here. I'll be glad when you all move out of my building. You kids'll be better off in an orphanage, I say. Your folks don't care about you. That's for sure."

Miralee stuck her tongue out at Mrs. Jefferson again. "You're a liar!" she screamed as she dodged the older woman's further assault.

"Now you kids eat that pizza and shut up. Mrs. Jefferson pointed to the remnants of the pie that she had scooped back onto the cardboard and replaced on top of the kitchen table. "I'm going downstairs and I don't want to have to come back up here again." She slammed the door as she left.

"Where we gonna go, Kenny?" Dottie clung to her older brother. "I'm scared." And she started to cry in earnest.

Miralee swallowed hard. "I don't wanna go to no orphanage."

Kenny wiped his eyes with the back of his hand, and then continued to portion out the remaining mass of pizza. "I don't know where we're going." His hands shook. "I hope Mama will take us with her."

The two older children ate joylessly in silence while Dottie continued to whimper.

\* \* \* \* \* \*

Custody is one of the major issues to be decided during

the process of divorce. Who gets the kids is of paramount importance to everyone concerned.

In recent times about 90 percent of custody decisions favor children living with their mothers. This is in contrast to prior historical trends where children almost always remained with their fathers. A child, categorized almost like property, usually belonged to the male parent in the family. In England, children had few rights and when they worked their earnings, too, were the property of their parents.

Later shifts in the views of society relegated custody of her children to the mother. That view is currently popular although many more children are beginning to make their permanent homes with fathers, even though most children still remain with their mothers after divorce. There is a considerable increase in the number of children who now live full-time with their divorced dads.

Divorce lawyers are quick to point out that the new change relates to the increased numbers of divorced working mothers. Women formerly stayed at home and cared for their children while the fathers worked. After divorce, the children continued to live with the mothers, because it was thought that the working father could not provide the needed attention to the children. Now with so many mothers also at work the old argument is altered, and either working parent can provide care depending on which parent is more interested and better at handling the job.

A New York friend described her brother-in-law's success in raising his three children. "He's the better parent," she declared flatly. "Even my sister Muriel, his ex, agrees that he's a wonderful father and is able to spend much more time with them than she could."

In *Divorced in America,* the author, Joseph Epstein, writes about his ex-wife's agreement that he should be the parent to assume custody of their sons following their divorce.

The parent who is awarded custody of the children decides the day-to-day questions. How often must Jane wash her hair? Can John stay out of school to see his Aunt Sara, who just came to town? Should Jane continue to see a pediatrician or is she old enough for the internist, etc.... The other parent is usually granted rights which may include visiting with the child certain days of the week, during vacations or school holidays, weekends together, or any variety of arrangements agreed upon at the time of divorce.

The courts usually try to decide custody primarily on the basis of what is best for the child, and the variety of arrangements differ from family to family, even though in most cases the children spend most of their time with only one parent.

Custody can be divided so that the boys go with the father and the girls live with the mother. Sometimes, if one child gets along better with one parent than the other, there may be only one child living with a preferred parent while the others remain with the other parent.

One Scarsdale family worked out just such an arrangement. The oldest son, who preferred his male parent, went to live with the father. The other two children remained with the mother.

Sometimes children will live six months with one parent and six months with the other. Or they may stay with one parent for a whole year and then switch to the other parents's house for the following year.

There have even been reports of children whose week is divided in half between two parents who live close to each other; three-and-a-half days with one and three-and-a-half-days with the other.

As in all other matters relating to divorce, the arrangements are highly individual and variations depend on the related circumstances.

In joint custody both parents determine the upbringing and education of their children. The houses or apartments of both parents are "home" to their kids. It can be called shared or split custody. Children go on living with both parents although the parents do not share the same house. Some families hope that a joint custody will relieve some children of feeling that they are divorced too.

Once in a while parents feel that it is easier for a child to accept the situation if there is a sharp break with the father or mother who will be absent from the home. In such cases the child loses complete contact with one parent.

There is divided opinion among the experts as to whether offering one or two homes is the best way to handle custody. Recently some authorities have begun to feel joint custody may be an innovative way of dealing with the living arrangements for children of divorce. But some child psychiatrists feel single parental custody is the least harmful to children.

Others disapprove. Certain authorities say they do not approve of joint custody because it is best for a child to have one home with only one parent, and visits should be arranged with the other parent to spend time together. These experts feel it is confusing for most children to have two homes.

Dr. Dorothy Kuhl, a psychiatrist from Oakbrook, Illinois, states that older children need one home as peer relationships become more important. Dr. Kuhl also states that split custody in which, each parent takes one or more of the children, is becoming a fairly common arrangement. "However," she goes on to say, "the child given away to the father may feel abandoned by the mother. The reverse also holds true."

One of the ironies of the custodial court battle involves the visitation rights of the absent parent. Hysteria and endless arguments often ensue while time allotments are painfully determined by attorneys on behalf of emotionally charged parents. Sundays are discussed. Holidays are gnawed over. Hours of visits are proscribed and all but carved in stone only to have the participants back off once the arrangement has been made.

"It has to do with not wanting to give something up rather than taking care of children," explains Dr. Seymour Pastron. "Children are an object of which one parent tries to deprive the other."

The wife of a California dentist spent anxious months in court insisting on her rights to visit with the two sons she had left at home. The embittered dentist looked without favor upon his wife's rights to visit the sons she had abandoned. Finally he was convinced to accede. No sooner had the agreement been reached, than Gloria, the wife, lost interest. She was involved with the owner of a supermarket in a suburban area in the San Fernando Valley and she cited her working hours in the store to explain her inability to visit with her children.

Dr. Calvin Lewis, an Illinois psychiatrist, confirms that parents are more interested in being given the right to visit their children of divorce than in actually seeing them or being with them.

What is the best custodial arrangement?

"There is no best way," says psychoanalyst Dr. Martha Kirkpatrick. "There aren't any pat answers. Divorce is always painful," she continues. "There is no reason for people to feel that their lives should always be wonderful and pain free."

Each family is different. And each mother and father has to work out the best shared time with their children. If they cannot do it alone, then the courts usually make these decisions for them. But whatever the choices, consideration must be given to what is best for the children."

## Part 1 Chapter 6

## If Your Child Asks, "Won't I See Daddy (or Mommy) Anymore?"

**Children in a divorce situation can feel overwhelmed when they learn that mommy or daddy are not going to be living at home anymore. They cannot draw upon any other previous life experience to comfort their tremendous sense of loss. Confused and unhappy, they can only be fearful that they may never see the parent who is leaving, ever again.**

* * * * * *

"Elem followed me around all afternoon," Mike said to his soon-to-be divorced wife. He had been upstairs packing his books and papers preparatory to moving them to his new house. "He seemed scared to death that I would get away when he wasn't looking. For Chris' sake, I couldn't even go to the bathroom without having him follow me. What's going to happen when I move out?"

Sara had been silent during the recital of events. She had just come back from making some transitory arrangements of her own and she had left Elem with his father.

The child had always seemed attached to Mike. Even his name, Elem, was Mike's initials. Mike was never called anything but Mike, and their son was Little Mike, L.M. or Elem, as they had called him since birth. Now Big Mike was going to be in one place and Little Mike in another. Henceforth, there would be small likelihood of confusing them, but the name stood like an umbilical of letters weaving a cord to his father. Yet the father was going to live somewhere else. How to deal with the boy's adoration for his parent? Sara and Mike were going to divorce. It was almost a *fait accompli*. But how should they handle the small boy's hero worship for his dad without destroying him by their rift? It was a knotty problem.

Sara and Mike sat far into the night discussing Elem until they arrived at a solution. They agreed that Mike would move as scheduled the following week, but he would continue to come over every day. "I'll still spend lots of time with you,"

Mike reassured Elem. The first week after Mike moved out he was over after work every day, having dinner together as usual and staying until after he had kissed the sleepy figure of his son and had helped put him to bed.

Mike saw Elem every day of the second week, too, but took the boy to his new house a couple of times and showed him the play area he had set aside for him. Elem was fascinated with his small alcove off the dining room.

Each succeeding week the father's visits were shortened slightly until finally he skipped a day but spoke to his son by phone instead. Sara had wisely arranged for a friend of Elem's to stay to supper that night.

The visits with his father were always enjoyable and Elem never felt the relationship slipping. Eventually Mike's visits tapered off to the two times a week that had originally been part of their separation agreement. Later, they even brought about a gradual introduction of a new name, Michael, so that when the boy developed a sense of independence even his name would denote an identity of his own.

* * * * * *

How wonderful it would be if all of us could handle the problems of divorce and separation as easily and as gradually as Mike and Sara handled theirs and Michael's.

Generally, children tend to have a more delicate and intense kind of relationship with their mothers than they do with their male parents. However, it is not unusual for preschoolers to worship the huge male figure in their lives who whips them high into the air and lets them see the world from the heights of his broad shoulders.

The relationship becomes more challenging as a child edges toward the school years until he or she reaches maturity. Gradually, aggression creeps in. How many of us have watched our children grow from clinging, adoring offspring to charging teenagers who are certain they are on the verge of unlocking the secret of human understanding that has been denied these unthinking people, their parents.

Although a boy's or girl's feelings for the mother usually are intense and variable, children also can be easily upset in their relationships with their father. A father's role, supplementary to the mother's, is uniquely different. Dad is the one who *heads* the family with a sense of firmness that brings stability and security to the children.

He's the one mother turns to as an arbitrator for unacceptable behavior. "I'll tell your father about this!" or "We'll see what your father says," echoes the length and breadth of the land. It may sound threatening, but unless carried to extremes, the effects upon children are quite opposite. It makes them feel cared for and loved having authority figures who evaluate their behavior and always watch over them.

At the same time it can be rather special to spend extra time with dad. Even in these days of redefined parental roles, and on overlapping of what was once considered male or female family chores, dad stands alone in his own relationship to his children.

A young high schooler explained her feeling when her mother went to Minnesota to visit their grandmother and left the two children at dad's home, which was nearby. "It was really great. Dad did the barbecuing each night for dinner and I made the salad. Eddie's job was to scoop out a different flavor ice cream for dessert. And one night we also had Eddie's chocolate chip cookies that his class made that day. They weren't bad for a 10-year-old boy! All in all, it was like a picnic for a whole week." Time alone with dad seemed like prize time, too.

But what happens when a child faced with ensuing divorce in the family worries about whether he or she will still be able to spend time with their father? Such a child may feel threatened with abandonment. Dr. Calvin Lewis, a psychiatrist, explains that the child may think, "If Dad left Mom and me maybe now *she'll* leave me too!" It's important to reassure your child that he or she still has a mother and a father and if there have been any concrete times set aside for visiting with the absent parent, these should be made known to the child.

For instance, you could say, "Mommy is going to spend every Saturday afternoon with you." And you can explain in detail how the child will prepare for the visit. Perhaps the other parent can detail what they may do during their visiting times. The father who is going to spend Sundays with his child can assure his child by telling the children what they are likely to do in advance. As time passes and the child understands that this new routine does not mean he will not see his father anymore, he will come to feel much more secure.

What, however, should you do if the other parent who is to visit does not live up to his commitment? Supposing you have both assured your child that your divorce will not alter his meetings with dad and now suddenly you find that dad has ceased to show up for his time with your son or daughter. Try not to blame the other parent but do not cover up for him either. It's best to take the bull by the horns and admit the problem without assigning blame to anyone. Explain that the other parent sometimes has a problem living up to his promises and that it has nothing to do with your son or daughter. Tell your child that this situation is not likely to change and he will just have accept the fact that things will always be indefinite with this other parent. Perhaps you can tell him that other children, even some who grew to be famous, had fathers who did not visit.

Gerald Ford, former President of the United States, had a biological father who never visited him after he was about 2 years old. When his mother remarried, young Gerald assumed his stepfather's name, Ford. He didn't see his real father again until he reached adulthood.

How the members of any family react to change, is a very individual matter. Each situation varies with the age of the children, whether or not there are brothers and sisters, what the relationship is with the siblings, how secure a child tends to be, how troubled he is by the change etc....

Sometimes a father, involved with long working hours, may find himself in a position where the child will actually be spending more time with him following divorce. For instance, if he usually worked nights and slept days his child might have gone for long periods deprived of his companionship. But if a divorce agreement includes Sunday afternoons with Susie or Tommy, these children may be having more contact with this parent than they even had before.

Sometimes fathers never extend themselves to develop any kind of close contact with their children because they leave it up to the wife to *see to the kids*. After divorce, the father will suddenly focus his interest on the children. It's almost as if he is just discovering them and doesn't want to lose out on his share of the offspring. That's all to the good. When such a father seems almost to want to prove to the world and himself how good he can be at the job of *fathering*.

What to do with your children when you are spending time with them? Don't fall into the trap of acting as if it's a vacation visit. It's all well and good to take your kids to the ball

# DADDY DOESN'T LIVE HERE ANYMORE

game and out to some special restaurant but this is not necessarily going to build a firm bridge between you and your children. The temptation is great to do just this.

The full-time parent has to deal with the mundane, everyday aspects of the child's life: getting his shoes repaired, going to the laundry, cleaning up the mess that was made in the kitchen and insisting that the child share in the chores, etc.... How natural for the part-time parent to want to put himself or herself in the fairy godfather or godmother role and be the giver of good times. Each parent wants to be the *winner* parent vis a vis his children.

Everybody's life needs a little sweet frosting but no one gains from an unreal relationship. A natural situation will contribute more to a sense of well being. When your child comes to visit, let him share your life. If you're putting up some shelves in the basement, let him help you. If your child is too young, let him make a game out of handing you the hammer and the nails. Let him help you measure. Let him hold something for you. In short, let him live your experience with you. At the same time, live part of your child's life too.

It is unproductive for a child to bring her school theme over to dad's and have him do it for her, but many common interests can grow out of sharing a child's project.

Suppose a school report relates to a certain type of prehistoric animal. There is no reason why a visit to the museum should not preceed or grow out of such a study. Perhaps you can go to the library with your daughter and get special slides on the subject or help her look up related material that will aid her writing of the report.

If you are asked to look over the finished product, add a word of encouragement. Help your child with love and interest but let her develop her own sense of responsibility and self reliance.

It's a very good idea to spell out visiting times in definite terms. It's much easier to have it all down in writing than to *assume* that it will work out. If your ex-husband or ex-wife decides to move and you have not had a firm visiting agreement, you are apt to involve yourself in costly bills trying to reach your child in his or her new location. Or it may make visiting totally impossible for you at all.

A large percentage of the kidnappings that occur in the U.S.A. each year result from child snatching by a mother or father who failed to obtain custody in a divorce and are dissatisfied at not being able to visit their children.

Both mothers and fathers are important to the best development of children so reassure your child that you will continue to be his parents and will see him even after divorce.

## Part 1 Chapter 7

## Does It Make a Difference if Your Child Is Adopted?

**Children of adoption usually are aware that they have once been discarded. For whatever reason, they did not remain with both biological parents. Will your child translate your divorce as disapproval by another mother and father? How will he handle the trauma of being a child of divorce when he is already burdened by the knowledge that he is adopted?**

* * * * * *

He heard Miss Nelson explaining the arithmetic but he just couldn't keep his mind on fractions. What difference did it make to him? His problems were ten times worse than figuring out the arithmetic.

Jeffery put his head down on his desk and closed his eyes. What was going to happen to him now that Mom and Dad were going to divorce. Was he going to be given away again? No matter how many times Dad and Mom had told him he had been their chosen child, way down deep he had always felt that someone didn't want him at the start. Otherwise, how would he have wound up as an adopted child?

"All right, class," Miss Nelson's voice cut into his thoughts. "We're going to have a special project for Mother's Day. We'll get back to the arithmetic tomorrow. Now we're all going to draw a picture of our mothers and how we see her in our minds."

How did he see his mother, his real mother? He didn't know. Did she look like him, with curly dark hair? His other mother had straight red hair. So he drew his mother, the one he couldn't remember and he made her look as much like himself as he could. Why, why had she given him away? If he had stayed with his own mother he wouldn't be having this awful fear of not knowing where he was going to go. But she hadn't wanted him either. Or maybe she just couldn't keep him. He hoped with all his might that she had loved him and had wanted him but just wasn't able to keep him with her.

Again Miss Nelson interrupted as she collected the drawings. "Class dismissed for recess," and she added, "Jeffery, will you wait, please. I want to talk to you."

Now he was going to catch it, he thought to himself. He fidgeted as he walked up to Miss Nelson's desk and waited for her to gather the rest of the drawings.

She picked out his drawing and examined it as she sat down. The teacher was silent for a minute before she spoke. "I used to wonder if I looked like my real mother too," she said. "I'm also an adopted child." And she began to tell him how she had felt when she was a kid; how she would look at other children and never feel exactly like them no matter how good her mother and father had been to her. "Something was different about me and I knew it all the time," she explained. "I always felt like I was second best."

Jeffrey was amazed. How could she know that he felt exactly the same way! She seemed to understand just how it was. And she understood how awful it was now that his parents were going to get a divorce.

"Your mother came to see me yesterday," Miss Nelson explained. "Your parents love you very much! Your mom wanted to tell me they know how hard this will be for you, especially since you've been having some problems at school."

Gee, Miss Nelson was so nice, Jeffrey thought as he returned to his seat. They had talked all through recess and she said they could do it again soon. He didn't feel great but he sure felt better than when he came to school this morning.

Miss Nelson held a book up before the class. "Let's discuss our chapter on the Civil War now." She had a nice smile that crinkled her nose.

Jeffrey turned to the page. This sounded like a much more interesting chapter, he thought.

\* \* \* \* \* \*

Adoption involves the legal begetting of new parents. A child may acquire another mother and father or he may be adopted by only one new parent. As someone else's biological offspring, he is chosen through legal devices to become the son or daughter of an adopting couple. Or he may be the natural child of a parent whose husband or wife adopts him.

Once adopted, parents are legally liable for the care and welfare of these children just as they would be for their natural offspring. In the event of divorce they must provide for their maintenance. Adoption has made them responsible for a child who was sired by another person.

Divorce brings a double indemnity to children of adoption and especially to the child where neither one was a natural parent. To understand its effects it is necessary to review some of the psychological problems of being adopted.

From the onset of his life such a child is in a fight for security. Very often he must come to terms with the fact that he is an illegitimate child. Furthermore, he knows at some level of his consciousness that he became a child available for adoption because somewhere, someone didn't want him.

"Divorce brings further insecurity to an already insecure child," says Dr. Pastron. The analytic point of view suggests that adopted children have many neurotic problems. Frequently they may not be good students in school because they are distressed by the strain of being adopted. This same kind of additional strain causes the adopted child to have more social problems than the nonadopted child is likely to encounter.

Despite the avowal of the adoptive parents that "You are our choice. We chose you to be our child," an adopted child is not a natural-born offspring. This is a fact that cannot be altered. He or she was not born from the body of the adopting parents. The adopted mother did not give birth to this son or daughter. They do not share the same genes. Often the decision to accept a child follows an inability to conceive which may leave the parents with a sense of inadequacy. No matter how often those who adopt may say they are now the child's very own parents the child knows that his real parents were someone else.

Adopting parents do make a choice. But any problems with the child of their choice may create feelings of ambivalence in them that will filter down to the child. Sometimes personal matters that do not relate to the child directly, such as feelings of inadequacy, cause a parent to feel regretful about having adopted. All these factors create additional strain and insecurity for the adoptee, whereas they could be more easily overlooked by a natural child.

"There is much more opportunity for things to go wrong with an adopted child,"says Dr. Pastron. "The interaction of natural children and parents is easier. The adjustment of natural parents and children to each other also is easier. Inevitability helps motivation."

But that is not to say that some adopted children do not

also make adjustment, however difficult.

A family in Georgia with a natural 11-year-old son, adopted a daughter of the same age who had been cared for since birth in multiple homes.

They were aware that the girl was a slow learner in school but after her first year with them they felt certain that Kate, the adopted child, was also retarded. They were somewhat regretful about having her, yet they tried to offer her every advantage. Their home was troubled at times by friction between the parents themselves and between the parents and children. However, the mother and father never divorced and as the children grew older they became genuinely fond of Kate.

After high school, the son, a bright young man, was enrolled in a fine university. Kate was sent to a private day school of limited academic standards. The parents went to great lengths to make Kate feel that Lee, her brother, was not the only one receiving all the family benefits of further education.

By now, the home environment had become much more stable. The parents' ability to get along had improved and the general atmosphere was better.

Kate's school entrance test were extraordinary. They showed her to have normal learning aptitudes. After a successful year at the nonacademic school she was able to enroll in college and later was able to enter a graduate program. It was found that she had never been retarded, only held back by many emotional problems that had gone unrecognized.

Some authorities feel there is a direct relationship between the age that a child is adopted and his later ability to handle complex adjustments such as a divorce by his adoptive parents.

All aspects of adoption are not necessarily grim. There are psychiatrists who feel the idea of choosing a child is an exciting one and that this makes a child different in a nice way. The idea of choice is felt to be joyous. But regardless of point of view, most psychiatrists and psychologists agree that the adopted child feels he is *different*. Many professionals feel that being adopted is not more of a hazard than any other difference people may experience—such as being too fat, too tall or too black.

# DADDY DOESN'T LIVE HERE ANYMORE

Divorce augments the problems of the adopted. Children of adoption, always trying to develop a sense of security, may worry that their parents will give them up just as their biological parents did. With divorce there is destruction to the very family they have used as a security base and they feel rejected again, this time by the adopted father and mother. A child who is already on shaky ground may feel personal ruin.

The adopted child who is the natural child of one of the divorcing parents is in a less vulnerable position. One of his parents was already his very own and the chances are that he will remain with that parent. His position is not much different from any child of divorce who remains in the custody of one parent. However, he does have to suffer the loss of a parent twice over; once at birth and now through divorce.

Although the adoptive father who divorces his wife must provide support for all children of his marriage, he is not obligated to support any of his wife's children whom he has not legally adopted. His legal obligations relate only to the children he has sired and those he has adopted in the courts. Legal adoptions of a husband's or wife's children in a marriage account for a large number of the adoptions that take place each year.

A decision to divorce creates a loss for all children and especially for children of adoption, who may have an especially difficult time adjusting to this new shift in family patterns.

After divorce, a parent can do much to alleviate the malaise of the adopted child by creating a happy environment at home. Reassurance of love by both parents is needed. Not all adopted children have the same degree of discomfort following separation, but since they run a higher risk of feeling insecure from birth on, it's important to strive for stability. All children need to feel secure—especially adopted children of divorced parents.

## Part 1 Chapter 8

## If Your Child Asks, "Who Will Take Care of Me Every Day?"

When children become aware of the change that divorce will bring into their lives they often feel very insecure. They may ask themselves many questions: Who will take care of me if Daddy is gone? What if Mommy goes away too? What if I'm left all alone, who will take care of me then? Not knowing the answers, children can feel only a consuming fear for their inability to care for themselves.

* * * * * *

Ginny was having a hard time falling asleep. Angry voices floated down the long apartment hall. Ever since dad had brought her home from the movie her mother and father had been yelling at one another.

Even before she had left to spend the afternoon with her father, her mother had been angry. "Wait till I get hold of your father," she had threatened. "Does he think I can take care of you with the few miserable dollars he gives me now?"

They had sent her to bed shortly after her return and now her mother's shouting carried into her room. "Thank God, you bought her a hot dog. I'm so short I don't know what we'll eat for the rest of the week." She could picture her mother's pink face.

Then her father exploded. "I can't give you more than I'm making. If you can't get along, go to work!"

"Oh yeah!" Her mother's voice snapped back. "And who will take care of the kid?" There was a pause. "If you're so smart, *you* take care of her. You take her and *I'll* go to work!"

Her father snarled his words. "You know I can't take her. We discussed it at the time of the divorce."

Ginny was terrified. They don't want me. Mom doesn't want me. I'm a lot of trouble to her. And dad doesn't want me. He said so. Her stomach felt tied in knots. Where will I go? What will happen to me? I'm just a little kid. I can't take care of myself. She shivered and sobbed into her pillow, but the noise from the argument in the kitchen was so loud they didn't even hear her. She lay there in a fetal position stuffing her whitened knuckles into her mouth and cried until exhaustion overcame her terror and she fell into a troubled sleep interrupted now and then by long, shaking sighs.

* * * * * *

It has been said that next to death divorce is the worst of human experiences. Children of divorce are a captive part of the process. Parents who decide, for one reason or another, to resort to divorce come to that arrangement after deliberation and choice. They institute the process and set in motion the social forces for disruption of their marriage.

The child, however, is a pawn. He has no choice in the decision. It is a totally undemocratic procedure. The children suffer harshly from the results and must be part of the arrangements that are decided for them. Their happiness marred, their security shaken, they must go along with the plan for separatism.

Such a child can become tortured with fear for his personal welfare. A child who truly feels that his parents no longer want him is helpless, lost and miserable.

But on occasion divorce can be good for a child. Some parents who formerly were very tense may become more relaxed with their children after divorce.

Under most circumstances of divorce children are apt to worry about their own welfare and to wonder who will take care of them after a decision is made to uproot the family.

Underlying such feelings are the fear of abandonment, a truly terrifying thought. Fears of being abandoned create feelings of rejection and consequently a sense of being unloved.

A tired young mother related her irritation at her three-year-old son who refused to come in for lunch because he was so engrossed with a game he was playing outside. After calling him repeatedly the exasperated mother said, "Very well then. If you won't come in now, I'm going to lock you out of the house and you'll have to stay outside." With that she banged the door shut and bolted it.

Her son, suddenly attentive, ran up to the door. He was

certain his mother was punishing him but didn't really mean the threat, so he knocked hard and declared with good humor, "I wanna come in now." "No," said the mother, "you were naughty and didn't come when I asked you to, so now you cannot come in any more."

The son was terror stricken. Where would he go? What would happen to him? "I won't do it any more," he screamed. "Please, please, let me in!"

Fortunately, the mother realized her son's intense anxiety and opened the door to receive the tear-stained child into her arms.

"What a stupid thing that was for me to have done," she admitted to her husband that evening. "Both of us would have been better off if I had gone out and walloped his behind, but punishing him that way could have been really destructive. He was *so* terrified that he would be left with no one to care for him. I'll never do that again!"

The incident was of such short duration that there was no harm done, but children instinctively feel vulnerable and know that they are dependent upon adults for their well being. They know that as young humans they cannot care for themselves.

Fear is a defense mechanism. It's an emotional condition that appears when there is a threat of danger. If a heavy rock is thrown at us, we recoil in fear, recognizing that we are in danger of being hurt. It's an automatic response that serves to keep us out of harm's way. It causes us to duck the impact of a heavy rock. Usually we have a concrete idea of what we fear when we are fearful.

Anxiety, on the other hand, makes us uneasy and uncomfortable. We also feel afraid but we are not certain why we are fearful. Children, worried about their welfare as a result of parental divorce, are usually anxiety ridden. Long-term conditions of anxiety can lead to grave emotional problems for a youngster.

Frustrating a child already worried about divorce is harmful. It serves to make him feel he is an unacceptable outsider. At times everyone feels frustration, but children who are harrassed for great lengths of time are almost certain to head for problems in the process of growing up.

Children should not be compared unfavorably to others. "You're not as good a player as Johnny. You never catch the ball." Putting someone down with sarcasm or constant discouragement and adding frequent punishment contains all the necessary ingredients for a highly troubled being; and more especially so for a hurt, bewildered child who fears for his own security because of divorce.

What can be done for a child who is worried about his security in the face of his parents' separation? Stifle the temptation to threaten your child with abandonment, no matter how tough the situation is for you.

You have to assure a child who is worried that he will always be cared for. You must stress continuity of care, psychoanalysts say. Tell the child that there will *always* be someone to take care of him.

Explain to your child that if anything should ever happen with his father or mother, there are grandparents or cousins with whom he could live. If there is no one in your family to whom that child could turn, explain that almost all towns or cities have special homes for children who don't have one of their own, or lists of people who like to take kids into their own homes. All these children are provided with food, clothing and shelter. It is important for each child to know that no matter what is happening to his own family he will not wind up in the cold streets without a place to go.

Many circumstances besides divorce can cause children to worry about being abandoned. One couple whose family business caused them to travel a great deal insured their children's emotional security by writing a will stating that the mother's brother and his wife would raise their children in the event of some major common disaster. Their children knew about these arrangements and understood that they were always going to be in the care of loving family members.

Frequently parents, alarmed over such a possibility, refuse to travel on the same plane. It's not unusual for husbands and wives to follow each other on consecutive flights to their destination in order to avoid a shared accident that would leave a child parentless.

A distraught child who worries about divorce should be reminded that he will not always be a child and that ultimately he will grow up and be able to take care of himself. It can be pointed out that he will be able to take care of others, perhaps his own child or another child who is in need of care.

It is important to allay the fears of aloneness of a child who feels no security. Reassure him.

The problem of being bereft has always been a favorite topic in literature. Charles Dickens wrote often of children who had no family. A popular comic strip is called *Orphan Annie*. The idea of being alone has troubled every human being and holds universal interest.

In the last century, English children who were left orphaned were stigmatized. They had no worth in the eyes of society of that day and were sometimes treated as slaves. So important is the sense of belonging, that *Roots*, a book by Alex Haley, became an instant success when it portrayed the search for origin of one black family.

Whether or not one can trace his own roots, society no longer stigmatizes anyone who has been orphaned and raised in public or private institutions. On the contrary, honor is accorded those who have overcome such handicaps and gone on to achievement as did baseball great, Babe Ruth.

During the process of growing up, most children will wonder if they were orphans. Am I really my parents' child? children may ask themselves. The psychoanalytic concept describes this as a complex way for a child to handle ambivalence towards his parents. A situation may arise that creates thoughts of hate. The child loves his mother and father but feels guilt at having such powerful feelings of anger and hatred towards one or both of the two most important people in his life. In order not to be preoccupied with his mixed feelings toward his parents, the child subconsciously suggests to himself that he's an orphan and these people, his parents, are strangers. Thus he can feel free to hate without guilt.

Don't ignore a child's concern about being abandoned after divorce. Emotional coldness can be destructive. Too much affection can be stifling. Constant reassurance is best.

Better yet, anticipate the possibility of such fears. If you're going to divorce, understand that it is quite natural for your child to wonder what will happen to him and to worry about who will care for him. Be sure to tell him right off that he has two parents and that he will always be cared for. Explain and explain again if your child seems troubled. Try to explain his fears away until he feels more secure.

## Part 1     Chapter 9

## "What if You Get Sick or Die? Who Will Take Care of Me Then?"

**Fears.** Divorce creates personal fears in many children. They may envision themselves wrenched apart from their separated parents. Having one parent gone from the home they may worry about a future in which the at-home parent will sicken and die, leaving them alone and unattended. They can only wonder what would become of them in such an instance.

\* \* \* \* \* \*

"Mavis is going to stay with us for a few days," Jeff's mother said.

"How come?" He looked up the ladder at his mother who was hammering the window frame.

His mother climbed down and sat on the floor with Jeff. "Mavis's mommy has been very sick for a long, long time and now she has died. She was so very sick that she could not get well."

Jeff seemed to digest what his mother was telling him. "Who is going to take care of Mavis now?" he asked. "Won't she have a mommy any more?"

"I don't know what her father will do yet." She kissed the small boy and hugged him. "Don't worry about it. I'm sure something will be worked out." She climbed back up the ladder, and continued to work.

That afternoon Mavis and Jeff played funeral in the back yard. They buried Mavis's old doll. "We need a box," Jeff said. "They put you in a box."

"Let's pretend there's a box." She pulled some twigs from a nearby bush. "This could be the box." She sprinkled the broken twigs over the doll as it lay in the shallow depression. Then she started to cry.

Several months later Jeff's mom and dad told him that they

47

were going to live in different houses. The boy seemed strangely silent when he was told the news. For days he was frightened and nervous. Finally his mother sat down with him and tried to talk about the divorce.

"You're still going to have a mommy and daddy. We'll always be your mother and father even if we are going to divorce." She hugged the boy.

Suddenly he blurted out, "But maybe you'll die. They put you in a box and then I won't have anyone anymore because we're divorced."

Jeff's mother sucked in her breath. Could that be why her son had seemed so ill at ease, she wondered. She knew she had to put his fears to rest. "People don't get sick and die because they are divorced. That has nothing to do with it," she explained. "Mavis's mother died and she wasn't divorced. People sometimes become seriously ill and die. It happens to married people and it happens to divorced people." Then she went on. "Daddy and I will always take care of you just as we always have before. If something were to happen to either one of us, Grandma would love to have you live with her. So you see, there will always be someone to take care of you no matter what may happen to us."

"But what if Grandma dies?" her son persisted.

"In that case Aunt Norma and Uncle Ben would want you."

Jeff listened for a minute. Then he said, "I like their dog. He's a good dog."

That seemed to end the conversation and, thereafter, Jeff seemed less frightened of the impending divorce.

* * * * * *

Although we live in a world where violence and death are portrayed on television and watched every day by millions of children, actual fears and ideas of death are far different. Children may describe death as anything from a withered plant to a squashed bug on a sidewalk. Or it may be described in terms of an old worn-out person. But however it is described, it is frightening.

Children at about the age of 6 may worry that their parents will die and there will be no one to care for them. By about 11 those fears may turn onto the child himself and he will then worry that *he* will die and there is no quarter where he may run for security.

# DADDY DOESN'T LIVE HERE ANYMORE

A friend who grew up in an unhappy household described how as a young child she worried daily about dying. She used to make bargains with God from one holiday or occasion to another. She would pray to remain alive until her birthday, and from that time it was another bargain to last until Christmas etc . . . . And so it went until she grew older and became more concerned with living than with dying.

Where divorce is involved, children have to be reassured if they worry about parental death. They visualize death, like divorce, as losing a parent. Once again, a child is concerned about his own safety and security and he feels threatened by the rupturing effects of divorce. He fears his vulnerability. He is defenseless and is afraid that he will be left alone in a harsh world.

Parents would be well-advised not to threaten a child who is uncomfortable about death and divorce with chance words said in anger. Parents, too, are in a period of change and are apt to be irritable and short-tempered, so it would not be unusual for an unhappy parent who is having a bad time with an irritating child to threaten, "I can't stand your behavior any more. You're absolutely killing me." All you are doing is making your child more uncomfortable, and possibly creating problems for him and for yourself.

Sometimes children worry that death is a kind of punishment. If they have heard a lot of arguments in an unhappy household, they may worry that death will occur because one or both parents are bad and are deserving of such an end.

Perhaps a child reacts to the conditions in his house and also has been mean and contrary. Under such circumstances he may feel that his is equally deserving of punishment and will worry greatly about his own death. Children who worry about punishment by death because they've behaved poorly or have had unkind thoughts must be reassured that wishes and thoughts are not deeds and actions and that bad thoughts about anything do not translate into happenings. A child has to be told that everyone becomes angry at times and thinks bad things about others, but that this does not in itself cause bad or evil. In other words, just wishing won't make it happen.

One of the obstacles to successful parenting is that we reflect our backgrounds in dealing with our children. Parents who have lagged in developing their own emotional maturity are sometimes unable to behave constructively toward their children. Those who try to understand themselves are usually more conscious of improving their children's emotional lot.

Trying to understand what hurts children in terms of parental hang-ups sometimes requires emotional detective work by professional helpers.

One such case involved a child who seemed angry and unconcerned about others. His mother complained about him and was furious at his lack of cooperation with her efforts to maintain a clean and tidy home. Professional counseling showed her child to have a deep seated feeling of being unloved. The mother was an anxious and domineering woman exacting in her expectations from her child. She nagged him about keeping his room neat and then bragged about her maternal ability. She was certain her fixation about order showed her to be a marvelous mother who worked hard at housekeeping because she loved her child so much. Actually quite the opposite was true.

Later therapy indicated that she felt unable to love her child and tried to overcompensate by being a super mom who in effect made her child's life miserable. The child's angry uncaring manner was a reaction to his sense of feeling unloved.

Children need to establish good feelings with their mothers. Without such affection they may grow up feeling a lack of affection for anyone else.

Ideally we should bring our children up in a situation where everyone feels a place in the family set-up. If one parent is too authoritatian it may produce submissive or resentful children.

If a dictatorial father leaves because of divorce, a family may feel itself to be leaderless, especially if the mother in such a family remains a very quiet, passive parent. One of the children may have to emerge as the leader who replaces the absent father.

It is much easier for a family to adjust when the absent parent was a leader with the help and cooperation of the children and mother. Under such conditions the family would be more likely to function as a group and continue to function successfully even without the parent who withdrew because of divorce.

Up to now, society has been aware of some of the obvious effects of divorce upon the family, such as financial strain, but experts are beginning to study the emotional effects of divorce upon children and the aberrations that are produced upon the family structure.

If a child worries constantly about being left alone after a decision has been made to divorce, parents must ask themselves what is disturbing that child. If the divorce is imminent it may be just that; the oncoming divorce. But if such fears continue they may relate to seemingly unrelated occurrences such as the absence of a third person or someone who has been hurt. It may be many other things, in which case you should seek professional guidance.

Seeking outside help should never be looked upon as a confession of weakness or failure. Quite the contrary. It is no different from seeking other kinds of professional help. If we fracture an arm, we want to have care. Likewise, when we fracture a family, we sometimes need special care as well.

When our children worry about a loss through death or divorce, a mother or father must try to make them comfortable. This is often difficult since parents are usually distressed and unhappy at such a time. Bad as it is for them, it is even worse for children because they are unable to care for themselves.

It helps if parents try to listen to their children and to what they are saying. If the kids have failed in some respect, the mother and father can help by accepting their failure. Understanding and consideration are what parents want for themselves and what they should try to offer their children.

If children are left in a one-parent home as a result of divorce the father or mother should behave like a parent. Seeking friendship from their children, parents should not try so hard to be "with it" that they behave like a chum. Children need guidance from parents who offer them their best parenting ability.

In the event children grieve sincerely for the missing father or mother whose absence is felt because of divorce, let them grieve or mourn. Let them get it out of their systems. Let them cry for the other parent who is really gone from their family circle.

But don't let your child conjecture that because mom or dad is gone the other parent may get sick or die and leave him all alone. Assure him there will always be someone who will care for him and about him. Explain it until he or she is satisfied with your explanation.

## Part 1   Chapter 10

## If Your Child Asks, "Can I Keep My Pet?"

**Divorce creates a need to divide a shared life and all its appendages. Assets must be separated and furnishings are reassigned. Children's lives are arranged and even the future whereabouts of a family pet must be decided by the divorcing parents.**

* * * * * *

Joe and Mary Ann were having a none-too-quiet discussion about the division of property relating to their divorce.

"Edgar! You can't take Edgar." Mary Ann stared at Joe.

"What's that about Edgar?" His tone was bellicose. "He's my hunting dog. I suppose you think I'm supposed to give him up to you too?" He shooed a long-haired cat away from his chair. "Anyway, you've got Phoebe. Never liked this damned cat you got from your sister."

Mary Ann persisted. "But Andy. What about Andy? You know how attached he is to Edgar."

"Tough! You could have thought about your son's attachments before you decided to divorce me. He's used to me too, you know, and he's going to have to get along without *me* every day, so I guess you'll work out the absence of a dog the same way you fixed it up about me."

"You're impossible," Mary Ann raged. "Always were." She shuddered. "I've never been able to discuss *anything* with you." Andy, aged eight, charged through the side door. "Where's Dad? I saw his car outside," and he ran to his father and hugged him.

"Your dad came to pick up some of his extra things." Mary Ann paused. "And to get Edgar." She looked away from the boy.

"Edgar! Dad, are you really going to take Edgar?" The boy was obviously downhearted at the possibility.

Joe patted the youngster's head. "Son, I'm sorry. Edgar isn't just a pet. He's a valuable hunting dog and I'm going to kennel him near Pheasant Creek."

Tears ran down Andy's cheeks. "Please, Dad, please, Dad,

don't take Edgar away from me."

The father seemed determined. He turned to the large flop-eared dog who lay in the corner watching them from under his sad, heavy lids. "Sorry, Son. I can't give up everything in my life. I'm really sorry. Someday you'll understand." He snapped his fingers at the dog. "Edgar, get your leash," he commanded.

Andy intercepted the rising spotted dog. "Stay here, Edgar. Don't go with Daddy, please."

Mary Ann spat out at Joe. "Just see what you've done. Look at that boy. He's a wreck."

Joe, who for one moment had looked contrite and undecided, now hurled an insult at his wife. "That did it, Mrs. Big Mouth." He snapped the dog chain on Edgar's leather collar and started out of the room. "Get yourselves a substitute dog, a substitute husband and a substitute father." And he stalked out as Andy watched their departure through the front windows, amidst deep gulps and a pitiful storm of tears.

\* \* \* \* \* \*

A beloved animal is just one more being that a child may have to give up during the divisions made in a divorce.

Pity the poor child who becomes a pawn in family hostility. When emotions run high between the parents, they are least likely to concern themselves about their child's feelings or desires.

Often divorcing couples will quarrel over the disposition of pets, but as a rule household pets are assigned the same home as the children. Most of the time they remain with the wife. Of course, there are times when an animal will leave the house with the father, and if the pet was especially loved by the children, this becomes just one more great loss that the child must bear.

As many variations occur with pet custody as with children. Occasionally a father assumes custody of his children and the pets only to discover he is unable to cope with either. In one such case a husband had to return both the children and the pet to the custody of the wife. "I couldn't handle the kids and the dog. It was too much for me," he explained.

Alvin Becker, Doctor of Veterinary Medicine of Northbrook, Illinois, reports that some families will even add a pet to their household in the event of divorce. "The animal becomes a kind of substitute to fill the void left by an absent husband," he observed.

"There are many other reasons that a divorcing couple may *add* a pet to their household," continued Dr. Becker. "Frequently, a family feels a pet is a pacification for the children who are saddened by a traumatic split. Other times parents feel a child will learn to care for something or someone through being responsible for an animal."

Currently, most pets are dogs, although cats are becoming increasingly popular in our crowded and ecology-minded world. A cat requires less care and does not need to be walked. There is also no need to clean up as often after a cat, who can be kept more easily in an apartment or in a densly populated area. "In terms of I.Q." Dr. Becker explains, "the cat is the more intelligent of the two animals, but the dog is still popular because a human being can develop a more responsive relationship with it than with a cat."

Men and dogs have lived in a symbiotic relationship for at least ten thousand years. Early man and wild dogs found it mutually advantageous to share the hunt. Somewhere man discovered he could benefit by a dog's keen sense of smell and his herding instincts in rounding up other animals to be killed for food. The dog lived by the side of early man and shared his life. Pets continue to be a part of our lives.

Usually small children like larger animals. It has been suggested by many psychologists that youngsters may view their parents as a kind of large animal and thus will equate large pets with their parents. Older children, on the other hand, often prefer smaller animals. By the time a child is older he begins to emulate the parental role and feels himself to be a kind of symbolic parent to a smaller species. With this point in mind, a family may most often find it best to leave a pet to the care of older children.

Young children and young animals will share many common responses as they grow. Both are praised for good behavior and are scolded for unacceptable social patterns. Many children have grown up with a pet as though this were a member of the family, as in fact it is.

For years eminent authorities such as Konrad Lorenz have studied animals and birds, and as a consequence, much has been learned about the behavior of human beings.

Observations of depression in geese who have lost their

partners show them to react similarly to children who lack sufficient contacts with those human beings who are close to them. Frequently a goose without a partner will lose the courage to live alone and will take up a more active relationship with parents and other siblings. This hardly differs from the behavior of a divorced human who feels so bereft and lost that he takes up with sisters, brothers or parents to fill the void.

It is not at all uncommon for a dog to become depressed after the divorce of its owners. Anyone who has had a dog in his home and has noted the pet's unhappiness at the departure of a family member who leaves even for a short vacation will understand all too well.

Strange situations involving pets have arisen in divorce cases. One such case reported by Dr. Alvin Becker involved a dog-owning older couple whose children were grown and no longer lived at home. In the process of arranging a divorce they became so involved with finding a good home for their pet that they were unable to decide on custody for the animal. Finally they cancelled the divorce and decided to stay together for the sake of the dog.

Another unusual situation involving a pet-of-divorce related to an out-of-house father who continued to provide faithfully for his ex-wife, his children and their dog. As the pet aged, he deliberately added a younger dog to their menage so that the older one would have company. He also wanted to insure that his children would not be denied the pleasure of a pet should anything happen to the older dog. He not only felt he had to provide for the welfare of his ex-wife and children but for the dog as well.

Today's world is one of temporary relationships. People move around and make new acquaintances. They may have a constant flow of new neighbors. Their children go on to other schools where there are different teachers and new sets of friends. People frequently change jobs, meet new fellow workers of divorce and remarry. They may add new members to a family. Often the family pet may be a child's one object of continuity during his developing years.

With a loss of family following separation it is often helpful and offers security for a child who is attached to a pet to be able to hold on to this relationship. If at all possible the family pet should remain with your child after divorce.

## Part 1     Chapter 11

## "If Daddy's Not at Home Will He Still Help Me When I Need Him?"

Children fear the loss of assistance from a parent who no longer lives at home. How will I find him when I need him? they may ask themselves. Will Momma still help me as she always did before she went away? Who will brush my long hair? Who will fix my bike? The questions relating to parental helpfulness are endless.

* * * * * *

Peg looked at her watch. That had to be Trish at the door, home from school. "Just a minute," she sang out as she turned the key in the lock.

"Hi," Trish said as she stalked past her mother and flung her books on the table.

"No hello kiss for an old mom?" Peg chided her daughter.

Trish turned and pecked her cheek. "I'm sorry," she mumbled.

"Want some cookies and milk?" Peg ignored her daughter's long face. "I just made them, special. They're your favorite."

"O.K." Trish was unenthusiastic.

She had been moping like this ever since the separation. It's a hard transition for both of us, Peg thought to herself. At times she was almost regretful. Maybe she and Jay should have stayed together for Trish's sake. Maybe they shouldn't have filed for divorce. But, no! Even the thought of a lifetime of such unhappiness was unbearable. She couldn't have done that, either. But it was awful for the girl and she seemed more morose than ever today. Peg sat beside her. "What's wrong, Trishie?" She stroked her daughter's dark brown hair.

"Oh, nothing." Her daughter pulled her lower lip and then she blurted out. "It's Miss Kinzie. She said we should ask our fathers to help us with Unit 3. How can I ask my father? He doesn't live here any more." She was almost accusing.

It was time to face up to the facts.

Peg was loving but firm. "That's right. Dad does not live here anymore. But you still have two parents: a mother *and* a father. You can ask him about helping you when you see him."

"But I can't wait till next week!" she wailed, then brightened. "Mom, do you think I can call him at work? Dad gave me his number and said to call him if I needed to get in touch with him. Do you think it's O.K.?"

Peg tried to be honest. "I don't know. You can try." She looked at the girl's troubled face and hoped with all her heart that Jay would be receptive to a phone call.

Peg busied herself while Trish dialed. "Let him be pleasant to her," she prayed silently as she listened to her daughter's voice.

"Can I speak to Mr. Bauer?" Pause. "It's his daughter." Another pause. "Dad? It's me, Trish," and she launched into a nervous explanation of her call. There was a longer silence then a relieved, "You will?" And an ecstatic, "YOU WILL? She's right here, I'll ask her." Her daughter's face radiated pleasure. "Mom, can I go over to Dad's tonight? He'll pick me up right after work and he says we can get hamburgers and then he'll work on Unit 3 with me. Is it O.K., Mom?"

For a moment Peg felt a tinge of jealousy. She thought of the fried chicken she had been planning for tonight's supper. It would keep until tomorrow. She smiled. "Sure," she said. "That will be fine."

The girl hugged and kissed her. "Mom, you were right. I still do have two parents."

* * * * * *

Each parent has a different relationship with his children. In most homes children relate certain kinds of activities with one parent. Sometimes dad is the one who always takes the kids to the kiddie park on Sundays. Maybe mom is the one who always buys the children's clothes. Other dads help build things with the kids. Some parents share gardening experiences, museum visits or a visit to grandmother's with their children. There are a thousand little niches of family activities that come to be associated primarily with one parent even though the other parent may at times also share the experience.

A child may be concerned about who will assume the activities of the parent who is leaving the house. Because he is accustomed to the physical shape of his family he identifies certain areas of family life with each member. They may not all be pleasant identifications. Perhaps dad wallops the kids when they talk back or are naughty. Maybe mom only scolds the children when she's angry.

When a drastic change occurs in his home a child isn't able to think through the future; he cannot immediately understand that it's going to seem strange until he gets used to the family being restructured and there is a reassignment of the family tasks. Most often, he knows only that he is uncomfortable. If dad was the one who passed out the children's allowance every Friday after dinner, a child may wonder who will give him his allowance. If mom was the one who always helped with the arithmetic problems and she has left the house, a son or daughter may worry about who will help the next time there is a difficult lesson in addition.

The best way to anticipate such dilemmas is to arrange adequate visitation rights with the out-of-house parent after an agreement to separate. "Visitation is such an ugly term," one divorcee complained. "It reminds me of a funeral home, but on second thought, it fits the situation because it relates to the death of my marriage."

Children should be told what to expect after divorce. They should know that their absent parent will continue his responsibilities as a father if that is the case. It should be explained that even though one parent will no longer be at home to continue the duties of parenting every day, he will help whenever they visit with each other. It's best if children can feel that there hasn't been total loss of that parent.

A child who is apt to worry should know that the parent who is away is available to him. Establish a certain time or routine for visiting. Make it specific but with a degree of reasonable flexibility.

If Aunt Minnie and Cousin Dick are coming to town and the children are to see their relatives, either parent should be flexible enough to understand that such once-in-a-while happenings must be taken into account when it disrupts their scheduled time together.

If kids have been visiting with their out-of-house mother of father and are full of enthusiasm about the help they received, they should be allowed to talk about it. Even if the at-home parent has been miserably alone all afternoon, working very hard to scrub the house while the kids were enjoying their project with dad, the parent who stayed at home should squelch the green-eyed monster and curb the temptation to make any snide remarks. She should be pleased if the children still can turn to the other parent.

Children of divorce must be shared in the same way that a mother-in-law has to share her children. It's destructive for a mother to be unduly critical of her son's wife and it's not in the child's best interest for one parent to be hypercritical of the other, especially if that parent wants the child to feel he still has another parent who will assist him when it's necessary.

Ideally the main function of parents is to love their children and take care of them. They should offer them guidance and affection. A child whose parents have been divorced should know that he will still receive love, guidance and affection from both parents and that both will continue to take care of him.

A part-time parent can show responsibility for a child in many ways. Seemingly inconsequential acts can indicate love and concern. If a father knows his son is a model airplane buff and he sees a picture of a certain model plane in a magazine, that parent can show his feelings for his child by bringing him that picture. Or he can show special interest by making his daughter's favorite dish for her birthday dinner. It's not only the large areas of care, such as providing shelter and clothing that show a child he can count on an out-of-house parent. It's all the loving little things that people can do for each other that are so important.

It's different for the child where divorce is followed by a total absence of one of the parents. Sometimes the parent moves far away or simply drops his old family and goes on to another way of life.

Children who have lost their parents in such a way may worry about who will fill the job of fathering them. Grandparents can be wonderful in such a situation. Often they have more time and are more patient with grandchildren than they were with their own children. Not only are grandparents a bonus gift because they fill in for an absent parent, but they can be a tremendous source of comfort and an additional link to family roots. They can also add an important feeling of family continuity.

In the Soviet Union grandparents are a special addition to the family circle. Working parents have created a real need for mama and papa substitutes. Small children often are seen walking hand in hand with an older grandparent. Such children are secure in the knowledge that this is the next best thing to being cared for by their own parents. These loving grandparents are the unofficial baby sitters of the U.S.S.R.

Stepparents can sometimes fill the gap for a child who is missing one parent. Uncles, aunts or family friends can be substitute helpers too. Senator Ted Kennedy of Massachusetts seems to be just such an uncle. Since the death of his brothers, President John Kennedy and Senator Robert Kennedy, it is not at all unusual to hear reports of Senator Kennedy's involvement with one or another of his nieces and nephews. He seems to be the father figure for a large section of the Kennedy clan.

When does a child not need help from an absent parent? It varies from child to child. Infants are least likely to react adversely to the absence of a father. The mother is the most important figure in the lives of infants and very small children. As they grow and begin to need the father to show them other aspects of their world, children who have no adequate substitute are bound to miss a divorced father figure who is absent.

After divorce, a child's fears can be lessened by making him feel as secure as possible. Remind him that he has two parents to help him. Let him know when he can expect to see the absent parent. If the out-of-house parent is not often available, arrange for the child to maintain telephone contact with him. If that parent is going away for awhile or lives in another part of the country, encourage contact with letter writing.

Amy, a Chicago area child of divorce, was thrilled with the loving birthday card and a map she received from her father. "She needed the map for a school assignment so her father enclosed it with her birthday card," her mother related. "It meant so much to her that she could still count on him for help and he remembered her even though he now lives in Wyoming."

Parents who no longer live at home should maintain as

much contact with their children as possible. They should try to be available for any help their children may need from them during the years of their development. Even if that contact is broken, a child should be reassured that he still has one parent left and that there will almost always be someone else to offer him help when he needs it.

# PART II
# AFTER THE DIVORCE

# Part 2    Chapter 1
# How To Reorganize

When separation and divorce are a fact, the parents and children must reorganize their lives. They must accept the changes that occur in a broken family. Like chessmen they must rearrange themselves in relationship to each other and include the important parts of the old life in the new lifestyle that has to be developed.

* * * * * *

A new life. That's what she hoped it would be. Carol pushed some of her dresses over to Bill's side of the closet, or rather, to what used to be Bill's side of the closet. There was so much empty space in the drawers too. So much empty space in the rest of her life as well.

She felt so unreal, like it was happening to someone else. She tried to concentrate on her routine. She and her son would have dinner as usual at six o'clock. And maybe they could bowl a few lines after dinner. The long weekend loomed ahead. What would she do with all that empty time? Well, for openers she might call the singles group at her old church. She had run into a former friend who belonged and she had urged her to join. Maybe it wasn't such a bad idea after all. Her thoughts were interrupted when her son dragged into the room.

"Hi." His greeting was tepid.

"How was school today?" and before he had a chance to answer she added, "How did the teacher like your geography report?"

He removed his sweater and tossed it across the room. "It was O.K., I guess."

She tried to make a joke of the sweater and spoke directly to it. "Did Brucie bounce you a bit? Sorry about that. He just forgot. I'll fold you up so you'll feel better." And she folded the heavy green sweater.

65

Poor kid. He misses his father, she thought. He's got to reorganize his life too.

She tried hard to make conversation throughout their dinner. She was conscious of the fact that Bruce was trying, too, but both of them were acutely aware of the empty chair at the head of the table. He even helped her unbidden with the dishes.

As they finished Jimmy Patter from next door appeared with an invitation for Bruce to join in their family outing of miniature golf and to sleep over that night. Bruce was anxious to go. "Can I, Mom? Can I go?"

"Sure." She forced herself to smile. Why not? It was best to let him go on doing the things he had always done. That would make it much easier for Bruce. Carol swallowed as the door shut. It was worse for her with Bruce gone but she knew she had to let him go. Where did she belong? What should she do with herself? She only knew that her world had fallen apart. She didn't want to call any of the former friends that were hers and Bill's. It was awkward now that she wasn't a couple any longer and her friends were all in pairs.

She forced herself to find the phone number of the singles group she had been urged to join and dialed. "Hello?" She felt peculiar explaining who she was but before she had quite finished she received a welcome response.

They were having a meeting shortly. Could she come by? Several members lived in her area and she could probably go and come with them in the future, a friendly voice explained.

"I'm newly divorced. " Carol hesitated. "I'm not very good company."

The friendly voice was insistent. "Most of us are divorced too. You need us and we need you too. Please come," she encouraged her.

"You need us and we need you too." The words rang in her mind as she combed her hair and changed her slacks. To be needed. What lovely words! She would go. It sounded O.K. Anyway, it was a start. Maybe this would be a place to start her new life.

Getting yourself together after divorce is always difficult. Perhaps you are immobilized by a feeling of unreality and feel disorganized. Nothing seems real. Is this happening to you? Your world has fallen apart. Your companion is gone and has left a large void despite any unhappiness you may have experienced while you were together.

Your friends are evaporating. Some have taken sides and slowly you are aware of how strange a single person feels in a world of couples. It's as if the whole universe is in pairs and there's no place for an uncoupled loner.

You have to restructure your life. Where do you start? "Try to re-establish a sense of belonging in one place in the world," suggests psychoanalyst Dr. Seymour Pastron. "It can be through a church, it can come about with old friends, or you may find a new spot for yourself with a job, but whatever it is, you have to start to put down new roots in one place. As you re-establish a sense of *place* and a sense of belonging, you will begin to heal."

Whatever your own sensations, your children will be feeling a similar anguish on their own terms. They my be tearful and heavy-hearted. They may cry openly and be fearful and frightened. Reassure them that you are with them. If you know they will continue to see the other parent, remind them of that fact. Assure them that they are still loved by both parents and will continue to receive care.

Tell your child that you understand how unhappy he is because your marriage is ended. But remind him that his position as a son or a daughter is not ended. It is ongoing and continuous, and is a firm fact, just as your own divorce is also a firm fact that will not change and must be accepted.

Remind your children that, difficult as transition may be, they will feel happier later on, after they have made the adjustment to being a divided family.

Talk about your plans with your children. Try not to spring any major changes on them, like moving, without telling them in advance. You do not need to consult them or obtain their permission but do try to let them share some of the transitory arrangments that will affect their lives. If it is possible, and works for your family, perhaps you can make these changes together.

Making major alterations in their lives without telling the children makes them feel inadequate. They may even view it as a threat to their security and feel some sense of danger and yet not know how to handle what is ahead.

Very often, divorce brings about sharp financial changes. Be honest with your children without frightening them. If you are going to have to work, tell them so and discuss any major difference in your lifestyle without worrying them.

One divorced mother worried her children so excessively that her daughter refused her allowance. "Here, Mom," her daughter said, returning the small amount of money. "I know we're too poor now."

Her mother was shocked. "Who told you that?" she asked.

Back came the daughter's reply. "You did. You said we won't be able to do the same things any more."

When you reorganize the chores around the house that used to be dad's, try to include the children in the schedule.

If dad used to take out the garbage after dinner each night, maybe your oldest can assume that duty. Don't be punitive. Do it in the spirit of shared family duties. But where you must now assume additional responsibility, assure your children that the activities will continue but that you will now take over.

Insofar as possible try to maintain some continuity to your children's lives despite the absence of one parent. If you always had dinner at a certain hour, continue to eat together at such a family hour. It's a good time for exchanging news of each other's activities and developing an interest in what each one is doing.

If dinner was formerly a shouting match between the absent parent, yourself and the children, there's no need to say, "See, no more fights with your father! Isn't this nicer now that we don't have to listen to Dad yelling anymore?" Show, don't tell. Make these times quiet and pleasant, and the example will explain itself as a more pleasant lifestyle.

Absorb the activities of the absent parent but don't make a spouse substitute out of your children.... Don't tell your son, for instance, that now he has to be the little man around the house and will take daddy's place. He is not daddy. He is your child. He has his own place in the family scheme so don't try to make him into someone else.

At best you may create a feeling of exaggerated dependency and stop both parent and child from forming needed relationships at their own level.

Whatever you do, don't fall into the habit of taking your child into your bed at night. If your child is upset by the absence of the other parent, offer him comfort and security but do it without having him settle into the empty place in your bedroom. Your child is a person and should be considered as such. You have upset his life and a little understanding will be of great help in aiding him to adjust to your reorganized household.

Turning to children as spouse substitutes can create much mischief for your child. If the substitution evolves on an erotic level you may interfere seriously with his developmental attitudes toward his peers.

Don't make it a habit to kiss your children on the mouth with passion or stroke their genitals. Such behavior can cause your children to feel guilt ridden and confused.

Stay away from such practices, for example, as referring to your son as "my little lover" or addressing a daughter as "my adored sweetheart." You can show love and affection without unduly arrousing your child's sexual fantasies.

You should, in fact, show affection to your children. Do kiss them and hug them. Even a grown daughter or son will enjoy the loving contact of walking arm in arm with parents or having your arm around their waist. Touching is a warm and lovely way to make human contact and show affection. A pat on the head, a bear hug, cradling a hurt child or a heartfelt kiss on the cheek are the life blood that nurtures emotional development. What you do not want to do is show the kind of emotion that goes beyond the bounds of beneficial parental love and becomes eroticised.

Sometimes children who have formerly had two parents at home worry that the one remaining parent may be inadequate to continue caring for them.

They may even show resentment to that parent because of a feeling that the mother or father broke up their homelife by the divorce, or the resentment may show itself to the absent parent instead.

The increased number of divorces leaves more children in an insecure position in their homes because of the changes they encounter. The National Center for Health figures for 1976 show two million divorced people for that year alone. It has been estimated that twenty million Americans have had close knowledge of these divorces through association with family or friends.

If you're one of the two million persons who divorced recently, you will have to reorganize your life. You can best do it for your child by helping him maintain a degree of continuity in his own life and by keeping him informed of the changes that are coming.

For yourself, you must make a start with one group of people or one activity and start to carve out a new niche.

The parent who is no longer at home must do the same thing. Sometimes it is a good idea to let the children help the other parent get settled in new living quarters and aid in making selections. Although this is not the children's permanent home, it is nice for them to have a shelf or a drawer of their own in this home too. This little corner may give them a sense of belonging here as well.

## Part 2    Chapter 2

## Time Spent With the Parent Who Is Not at Home

When a mother and father separate, the child and the out-of-house parent have to work out the time they are able to spend together. During visits they must trade information about past experiences, future plans and all the little happenings of daily life that a parent and child must know to keep up full contact with each other. They have to condense their former relationship to fit this shortened time slot.

* * * * * *

Harry Bazar whistled as he shaved. He ran through the itinerary for the day. Today was his Sunday with Vicki and Lauren and he had his time with them all planned down to the last minute. None of this moping about for his kids. He wanted them to have a good time when they were with him. He tried to really entertain them.

"Let's see," he talked to himself out loud. "I'll pick them up at ten and we'll stop to see Mother for an hour. Then brunch at 11:30 at The Apple Cart." Of course he would have to stop for a few minutes either before or after today's visit to talk to Sara, his ex-wife. They always discussed the week's happenings together. Usually Sara complained that her allowance didn't cover the extra gym shoes that Lauren needed or that Vicki was going to start taking guitar lessons, but on the whole, they had everything worked out pretty well. No one could say that his kids were deprived for the rest of the day. After brunch they would watch little league for awhile. Then they would drive downtown for the afternoon matinee. After that they would get in a few lines of bowling and by then it would be time for dinner. If the kids felt up to it they could try a game of miniature golf before he would take them home. He sighed with contentment. Yes, he certainly was a good father to his girls.

There was time for a short talk with Sara when he arrived to pick up the girls. Nothing out of the ordinary this week. Lauren was going to need braces soon, but he was prepared for it. The girls dawdled getting their coats. Vicki, the youngest, seemed especially slow.

"Doesn't she feel well?" he asked his ex-wife.

"No, it's not that." Sara seemed evasive. "They want to talk to you. They'll tell you about it."

Harry was mystified. The girls were quiet almost all the way to their grandmother's house. "Come on. Out with it. What's up with you kids?" Harry prodded them. Then, with suspicion, "Is this something your mother put you up to? That isn't Sara's usual style but perhaps this once," his voice trailed off.

"Oh no!" Lauren blurted out. "We didn't even want to come today but Mom said you'd be so hurt if we stayed home." His daughter looked miserable.

Dumbfounded he looked from one to the other. "What is it? Don't we always have a great time together every Sunday? I knock myself out trying to find fun things to do together!"

"That's just it, Dad," Vicki was nervous. "We don't want to do all that stuff all the time. We just want to be together so we can do things like we used to." Lauren added, "We just want to be with you Dad, not keep going places. We don't even get to be in your apartment."

"And if we're going to Grandma's why do we have to run in and out of there? Why can't we sometimes just spend the whole afternoon with Grandma?" Lauren was trying to explain. "It's like you don't really want to talk to us, but just keep us busy doing things all the time."

Vicki looked up, tears overflowing her eyes. "We love you, Daddy."

Harry choked up. He drew the car over to the curb and bear hugged his two daughters. He could hardly speak, so overwhelmed was he by their sudden revelation. "I love you so much," he mumbled. Then straightening up with resolve he said, "We're going on a new regime. How would you kids like to cook brunch at my apartment?"

"Yeah!" the girls shouted as they headed for the supermarket to pick up the necessary items.

\* \* \* \* \* \*

Visits with the *other* parent can be too much of a good

thing when they evolve into over-planned forays of public entertainment. Rather than developing a good rapport with the father or mother who is no longer at home, a day or an afternoon that is overly full of visits to plays, ballparks and zoos can leave a child frustrated and longing for a real visit with this parent.

Most children are highly sensitive to the newness of establishing a pattern for the time spent with the absent parent after divorce, and they may try extra hard to develop a good relationship with the father they no longer see all the time. A father who runs his kids ragged with plans during their day together may sometimes not even be aware that he is indulging in activity overkill. Sometimes children may fear his displeasure and be fearful of alienating him so they will say nothing about their own anxiety. Occasionally a child will not even openly object to vacation arrangements or unpleasant visiting that is not really to his liking if he senses that his father will be irritated with his refusal to go along. Basically, the child does not want to do anything that will lessen his chances of spending time with a parent whose full time he has already lost.

Children have even been known to court their father's or mother's favor by trying to be interesting when they are together. This may even be done unintentionally at the expense of the other parent if tidbits are revealed that the at-home parent would perhaps have preferred not to have told the ex-spouse. Difficult as this is, an intelligent mother who gets wind of such an error and knows her child is working hard to establish a good relationship with the other parent is usually well advised to accept the foible so long as the child doesn't develop the habit of consciously tattling.

One handsome little fellow who was about to vacation for the first time with the newly separated father was asked routinely how his mother was getting along. "Oh, Mom's fine," the bright four-year-old replied. Then he added, "We have so much company now. Harry comes over all the time. And you know what, Daddy? He even sleeps in your bed." The father was piqued to find himself so quickly displaced but tactfully led the discussion on to a safer area of discussion.

When the story was related to the mother by a third party she resolved to be more careful of her future relationships, but she understood that her child was being conversational and was relaying to her husband what he thought was a family pleasantry.

The entire situation of a child spending time with the other parent is a delicate arrangement at best. If you are the home parent, you are the workweek mother or father. You're the one who says, "Wash behind your ears," and "Pick up all that junk I nearly tripped over last night." You have to scold, ask why he needs the extra quarter when he just got his allowance and make all manner of unpleasant decisions.

Then along comes the Sunday father with tickets for the ball game, a fun hour at his new home, and perhaps an expensive snack-type supper like spareribs or fried chicken that you can't afford, and your child comes home telling you how great it was that they ate from paper plates in daddy's living room while watching television.

On the other hand, the out-of-house parent worries about having his children feel comfortable in two households. The possibility of loosing contact with his children gnaws at him.

He is no longer a member of the child's primary home. He has lost his role as head of the family. If his wife is now working and adding to her own income and helping in the financial care of the children he may even have lost his position as chief provider.

There is a lack of shared continuity in the daily lives of his children. Conversely, the child no longer shares in hearing about the small details of his own life, like small pleasures or irritations that occur during his working hours. The child also cannot keep him abreast of these same kinds of happenings at school or at play.

The father is not on the scene when an immediate crisis arises. He may be painfully aware that he's not even around when danger lurks. Perhaps he was the one who formerly picked up the child after some very late activity. If the mother works, he may now have to face the fact that his child will have to come home alone at a dangerous hour or give up the activity.

The extent of primary parental responsibility toward a child depends on custody, but the extent of worry about that child's welfare depends on the individual. As mentioned in an earlier discussion on custody, the question of choice changes with social conditions. In the days when there was greater concern for property and the passage of property to rightful heirs, sons were considered as primarily of the father's house. The father wedded and bedded the mother but everything, the child, and the mother and her property belonged to him. Kingdoms and vast land holdings were passed in this same manner.

Literature has frequently portrayed the parental wrench of being separated from a beloved child while reflecting this societal view. Tolstoy's masterpiece, *Anna Karenina*, tells of Anna's love affair with Count Vronsky. When she goes off with the count, she understands that she is doing so at the expense of her relationship with her son. She knows that she cannot have her lover and her son too. Her husband denies her the right to even see her son. He, the husband, is master of the household, the son and all that goes with it. The father was supreme and Anna had no rights to see her child.

When children began to be viewed by society less as property and more as individuals, they began to be left to the care of the mother when there was a change in the family structure.

Presently the women's liberation movement has turned attention to the equality of the physical conception of parenting. Some males are beginning to seek custody of their children.

Other men are truly relieved when children are awarded to the mother's care. Their lives are in a state of confusion and they feel a tremendous sense of inadequacy when confronted with the possibility of raising their children single-handed.

Still other fathers feel this is another blow to the ego and yet another insult. Not only does he, the father, have to divide his money and his property with someone he no longer loves or even likes but now he must even divide his flesh and blood: his children.

Most frequently the disposition of *who gets the children* takes a variety of factors into consideration. The children's desires are considered by the courts, as well as the total family situation and the needs and abilities of the individual parent to care for the children.

One recent separation of a professional Georgia couple involved a lesbian mother who desired custody of both children. The father agreed that despite her sexual preferences, the mother could provide competent parenting. But the teenage son, fearing that his father had been victimized by his mother's aberration, pleaded to be allowed to stay with his dad.

Both parents worked hard to make the son accept the situation, feeling that it was important to the boy's own sense of well being to have some degree of understanding of the parents, warts and all.

Time spent with one's children has to develop an acceptable pattern for visiting. The parent and child have to play together, talk together, read, go places and condense a system for trading information that will permit them to stay in good contact with each other.

The father or mother has to listen to the children and encourage them to talk. The out-of-house parent has to work at trying to have the visiting child feel comfortable in this other home.

Despite the alteration that has occurred because of divorce or separation, the father remains important. He is still an authority figure and must offer direction, interest and love. A child always continues to need two parents.

## Part 2   Chapter 3

## Whose House Does the Child Go to for Holidays?

**Special occasions and holidays may present difficulties for the child of divorce. Wishing to be with both parents, he nevertheless must make a choice. He cannot be in two places at the same time. Parents and children have to try to arrange these times with consideration given to the individual needs of everyone concerned and through compromise.**

\* \* \* \* \* \*

Patty pressed her nose against the plane window hoping to still catch a glimpse of mom somewhere out there in the busy airport. But it all looked so different from inside the airplane and she couldn't see anything as the big vehicle rolled away toward the runway.

Takeoff meant taking off to her father, and Patty had mixed feelings about going. She hated to leave mom at Christmas time. Yesterday they had exchanged the gifts that sat under the tiny tree on top of a draped card table. Mom had cooked a small ham for the two of them and had tried to make their evening especially pleasant.

Last year she and mom had gone to grandma's for Christmas dinner, and Aunt Faye and Uncle Sam and her three girl cousins had driven in from Philadelphia to be there too. It had been so much fun being a big family for the occasion. They had popped corn and had a song fest with Uncle Sam playing grandma's old piano. Then Uncle Sam started to play rock and roll music and all the girls danced and even grandma waved her hands and stamped her feet in time to the rock. It had been great!

Patty felt so empty. This year grandma was dead and it was her turn to spend this holiday with her father and his new family who now lived in Los Angeles.

77

It seemed strange being at dad's after the divorce and his re-marriage, as if she was a visitor and didn't really belong. She always felt that she had to behave with her company manners. Helga, dad's wife, was O.K., and her son, Eddie, wasn't too bad either, but Patty didn't really feel that she knew them. This year there was a new baby, Holly, a sister that she hadn't yet seen.

Each time she returned home after visits with dad, it was strange telling about her holiday. She usually told mom most everything but this was different. Her mother was polite and didn't ask a lot of questions. Grandma used to ask more questions than mom ever did but Patty felt uneasy telling her mother about all the things they had done without her. Especially this year, it would be even worse knowing that mom was all alone. Grandma was gone and Aunt Faye and her family weren't going to be with her either.

The voice of the stewardess interrupted her thoughts. "Would you like beef stew or a hamburger sandwich for your lunch?"

The older woman next to Patty laughed. "What a question for a young lady! I'll bet she'd rather have the hamburger." Patty nodded. "And I will too. I'm Mrs. Baker," she introduced herself, looking at Patty.

"You looked like you were out in California already," Mrs. Baker commented. "For such a young girl, you seemed to be very far away in your thoughts."

Before she knew it, Patty was telling all about herself. About how she was almost 12 and was going to visit her father and how sad she was to be away from her mother. Mrs. Baker listened and seemed so understanding that it was easy to talk and talk. By the time the hamburgers came she had told Mrs. Baker many things. Patty wondered if she should have told all that stuff about the divorce to a perfect stranger, but somehow she felt better about it.

Mrs. Baker paused before taking a bite out of her hamburger. "You know, you're lucky," she said. "When I was your age, both my mother and father died in an automobile accident and I had to go into an orphanage. It wasn't bad there and we had lots of nice times but I remember how much I missed my parents. I would have given anything if I could at least have had one of them to visit."

"I've still got both of my parents," Patty answered. "I still *do* have them both, don't I?" She hadn't thought of it like that before.

Mrs. Baker smiled, "Of course you do. They may not live in the same place but it sounds as though they both love you. As long as they're alive, you'll always have two parents. And two families." Then, as if she'd asked herself a question, Mrs. Baker continued. "Yes, I'd say you're a very lucky little girl and you're going to have a great time in California."

Patty smiled too. Somehow she knew Mrs. Baker was right and she *was* going to enjoy her visit with her California family.

\* \* \* \* \* \*

Holidays can be especially grizzly for some divorced parents. There are certain times of the year that are identified with family and being together. Very often they involve large celebrations; eating together, praying together or exchanging gifts. Christmas is one such major occasion during which there is a social emphasis, a family gathering, festive dining, a religious spirit for those who view it as a spiritual holiday and an exchanging of gifts. An occasion that includes so many ritual and religious feelings is bound to be a time of difficulty for a shattered family that no longer shares the holiday.

Such a family must decide when and with whom the child will spend his time. If the festivity formerly included a special celebration, it has to be a sore loss for the child who can no longer be with both parents. A choice has to be made that will be most agreeable to the schedules of the parents and the child and one that permits a degree of flexibility should unusual circumstances arise.

One happily divorced New Jersey couple related that they had split the holidays evenly and that the children spent the time with each parent and their extended families on alternate years. For instance if one family took Thanksgiving the other took Christmas and the following year they switched.

Vacations should be planned so that the child who is visiting a remarried father or mother should not be made to feel like an intruder. The time should be so arranged that when the child arrives to share the holiday he can do so as a member of that family and not as someone who is interfering with prearranged plans.

If something occurs that causes a preplanned vacation or

trip together to be canceled, treat your child as you would anyone else whose opinion you value and whose honor and trust you would want to have. Explain the situation and make sure your child understands the reasons for the cancellation. Above all, make certain that the child knows that he is loved and is wanted but that the situation was beyond your ability to forsee.

In instances where children have to make the decision as to where they want to go, the wise parent will let the child decide and then abide by the child's decision. This is not always easy to do.

One Seattle mother who was suffering from a debilitating disease had to suffer in silence as she watched one child after another opt to spend holidays and other occasions with the divorced father who remained in good health.

Ultimately the mother's health became so poor that the children went to live with the father who had moved to another state. The situation was a cruel one for the mother but it would not have made the children's lives better to remain with the mother who was too ill to care for them.

The oldest child, who was 14, had a most difficult time determining where his duty lay. All too frequently the consequences of divorce bang up against problems that seem insoluble and it becomes necessary to simply develop the best possible solution, imperfect as it may be.

Choices must be made about all kinds of family occasions. There are religious holidays such as Easter or Passover to be considered. These may vary in importance with the individual family. Birthdays may become a sad occasion without both parents. The absent parent may be able to soften the missed togetherness by phoning or sending a letter.

National holidays such as Fourth of July may formerly have been the time for a family picnic or a barbecue. Once again a decision has to be made about spending this holiday with one parent or the other.

Often the major holidays are more difficult for the divorced parents than for the child. The parents may try very hard to make it up to the child. In fact, some children may even wind up with two Christmases and two Thanksgivings celebrated on alternate dates. But so often the children go off, and as in the case of the Seattle mother, a parent may be left all alone.

Very wealthy children run into their own brand of loneliness during holidays or special occasions. One can almost describe them, at times, as golden orphans. If their divorced families are involved with great social and business schedules, rich children are sometimes left to spend holidays in an exclusive boarding school because the parents are overly concerned with their own activities. Such children are even shunted off on special tours or to camps that cater to those who are left alone for holiday or vacation periods. On occasion an obscure relative may be dredged up to attend to the child during the holiday.

The end results are not so different from those experienced by disadvantaged children whose working or otherwise occupied parents shunt them off to stay with a casual neighbor or another disinterested party. All of these children must believe that they are the exceptions to a whole world of people having fun and that they are rejected and unloved, as well they may be.

Some psychiatrists suggest that when a child spends special times with a parent, the parent should adopt the most elemental way of showing love. Offer the children food. Unconsciously food equates with love and relates back to the function of nursing the newborn.

When a visiting child's favorite dessert is included in the Thanksgiving menu the parent is doing more than offering him a piece of chocolate cake. He is offering him love with every mouthful.

How do you handle graduations, weddings or bar mitzvahs? Many separated families will reunite for these special occasions so the child can feel the support of his parents as a family unit.

One Kansas City mother invited the father to attend her son's bar mitzvah although she had not seen her ex-husband for ten years. The boy had maintained a close relationship with his dad throughout the years. Despite the father's lack of contact with the mother, both parents felt that the religious occasion of their son's thirteenth birthday should be celebrated with both the mother and father in attendance as though the family were still intact.

There were formerly some feelings of opposition to having both parents and their new families attending a child's graduation. Divorce has become such a prevalent condition in our society that it is no longer unusual for this to occur. The important thing is for the parents to make an effort to be present at a special function relating to the child.

One young man from New York City looked forward to a multiplicity of parents at his wedding. The father had remarried three times and in each case the groom had maintained a good relationship with a stepmother who had since also remarried. His biological mother and her family were dazzled by the array of ex-mothers and spouses who showed up to her son's nuptials.

When any occasion arises in a child's life that calls for parental participation, such as parent's night at school, communion, graduation, etc., each one would be well advised to try to share the event with his offspring. It's one of the very important ways you can show your child that you really love him and that you're still a parent who can be counted on, even though you are separated or divorced.

## Part 2  Chapter 4

## What About Your Child and the Grandparents?

Grandparents can be highly beneficial to children of divorce. They usually have a genuine interest in their grandchildren, whom they often view as a reflection once removed from themselves. They extend a child's family circle and are additional members who can be loving and supportive of his needs.

\* \* \* \* \* \*

Nick paused in the doorway before entering. The scene inside the room overwhelmed him with gratitude and love. Amy, his youngest, clean and combed, was curled up in his father's lap. Tommy and Sue sat at his feet listening to a story of Grandpa's boyhood. He knew his mother was in the kitchen because he heard her movements and smelled the familiar cooking smells of his boyhood.

Just days before he had been numbed by a marital explosion that had shattered his life. Grace, his wife of ten years, had packed her bags and gone. Their marriage had never been great, but it was nevertheless a union. Despite the complaints and the arguments, they had been a family; he, Grace and their three children.

She had found someone else. She told him about it before she left, but not until last week had she felt impelled to smash their marriage and leave behind the three children; souvenirs of their years together.

Grace had never known the reality of taking care of the kids alone. He had always helped. Still, she had kept things going after a fashion. But her departure had bogged him down with soiled linens, cookie crumbs, T.V. dinners, dirty jeans and runny noses. Perhaps he could have handled it better at another time of his life, but with his emotions pulling him apart on the one hand and making him feel unreal and unfit and the children frightened and crying, he had been unable to cope.

He could hardly express his extreme relief and appreciation to his parents when they arrived. They had taken over like a firm, soothing breeze on a clear spring day, permitting him to catch his breath and pull himself together.

"Daddy!" Amy ran to greet him. "Grandpa's telling us the *best* story about when he was young and Grandma's cooking the *best* dinner."

"Wait till you see what we've got." The words tumbled out of Sue and Tommy in rapid succession. "It's your favorite."

"Grandma and Grandpa are going to stay here until we get a housekeeper." The relief in 9-year-old Tommy's voice was evident.

"That's great!" Nick tried to sound carefree as he answered.

He kissed his children in rotation, put his arm around his father's shoulder as he greeted him and made for the kitchen so he could hug his mother.

Everything was under control. He sighed audibly. "Thank God for grandparents," he said aloud.

\* \* \* \* \* \*

Grandparents add a wonderful dimension to the family circle. In times of distress they will often come to the rescue and take a more active part in helping with the grandchildren. They may care for the grandchildren or even support them. A divorce in the family is upsetting to grandparents just as it is to other members of the family, but being sufficiently removed allows them to function with a greater degree of calm and clarity. If the remaining members in the house pull together, it is often with the aid and comfort of the mother or father's parents.

Children of divorce sometimes make their temporary homes with grandparents during the reorganizing process. At such times some grandparents feel strongly that the grandchildren, as part of the family unit, must be protected and cared for.

Children, and especially small children, know they are vulnerable and fear for their own welfare when their family unity is destroyed. A child, fearful for his future, may find solace and security if he can feel that he has the option of living with his mother or father's parents.

Children are a gift to grandparents and grandparents are a gift to children. The boy or girl whose family network extends to include a grandma and a grandpa enjoys an added bonus. Next to one's own parents, there is no one whom one can rely on for unflagging and unstinting love as one often can upon the grandparents in the family.

"My ex-husband's parents baby-sit with my children whenever possible," a Chicago suburbanite explained. "My own parents are dead but Dick's mother and father have been wonderful to the children. They are loving and kind and have helped my children get over the hurts they felt after our divorce."

Increased longevity has created a wide range of ages in grandparents. Nowadays many are youthful in their outlook and understanding of the social changes that exist. Although they had more authority in former years, an easy informality is now possible that doesn't dilute the supportive aspects of the child-grandparent relationship.

Grandparenting is a second chance to enjoy parenthood minus the responsibilities. They have time and patience to enjoy the children, knowing that at the end of the visit they can return to their own more peaceful homes.

Children learn many valuable life lessons in their associations with the members of their extended family. It teaches them about continuity and the cycle of life. They hear about their past, and are able to imagine something of their future. They keep in touch with family traditions and learn the importance of the part they play in the group lifestyle.

Everyone sees something of themselves in other family members. Children, seeing their grandparents, see themselves reflected in a later stage of life. Old age become a reality when they kiss the wrinkled skin of a grandparent. They can learn caring and compassion by helping an ailing father's father. A small child who fetches grandma's purse feels needed and useful and ultimately recognizes the steps he is saving his grandparent.

Hearing a father or mother discussed by their father or mother brings parents down to an understandable size!

"Gee, I didn't know you hated to practice the piano when you were a little girl. Grandma told me all about it," a daughter told her mom.

The rivalry that exists between child and parent is absent between grandchildren and grandparents.

"My father was a wonderful grandfather, but he was only a second-rate dad," a son related. "He and I were always in competition with each other. But it is so different with my son and my father."

Change, which seems to the young as though they invented it, is seen in a different light when measured against the life experiences of grandparents.

"Why do you want to apply to a college in California," an Indiana woman complained to her son. "It's so far away." Her son countered, "How about your father! You've always told me how he came to the United States when he was fourteen and never saw *his* parents again. That was far away. I'll be close. I'll be able to come home for holidays and semester breaks."

Grandparents, being people, are not always problem free. A grandmother who is no longer in the childbearing age may have an unconscious feeling of being left behind. She may become intolerant and critical of her daughter. But after a divorce, she can be helpful with other children in the family, especially if the daughter remarries and a new baby arrives. An overworked mother can appreciate the supportive aid of her own mother, but it may be difficult as well if the mother interferes with a new husband or tries to impose her standards for raising the daughter's children.

Divorce and remarriage add stepgrandparents to the family tree. Sometimes remarriage may bring worries to a grandparent who fears losing contact with a grandchild.

When a son remarries or a daughter dies, often it is the grandparents who go to court and battle the remaining stepparent for the child's custody. In such cases they may feel that the child belongs with blood relatives.

Stepfamilies can become very confusing with their array of "his" and "her" relatives. Giftgiving occasions can also be sticky when grandparents send presents only to their biological relatives and omit the other children in the household. Generally most stepgrandparents tend to develop pleasant relations with all the children in a family.

It's wise to encourage visits with your children's grandparents, no matter whose side of the family they come from.

"Wife number one won't permit my mother to visit our son in her house," an Iowa actor complained. The actor who had a child by each of his first two wives, was incensed that his first wife should let her pique deprive their son of visits with his grandmother.

A child learns much from a good relation with a grandparent and loses much if he does not enjoy that kind of contact. In most cases children should be encouraged to enjoy the family extensions of their own mother and father.

## Part 2 Chapter 5

## If the Other Parent Says Nasty Things About You to the Child

Divorce creates feelings of anger between parents. The child, wanting and needing to love both, is often frustrated and ill at ease when he is bombarded with the bad mouthings of one parent toward another. He is caught in an emotional vise of discomfort with which he is unable to cope.

* * * * * *

"How's my boy?" His grandmother caught 4-year-old Bobby up in her arms. "Did you have a good time with your dad this afternoon?"

Muriel, Bobby's mother, kissed her son too. "Where did you go with your father today?"

"Oh, we just went around to different places. We were going to go to the zoo but Erna said she felt too cold to be outside that long."

"Who is Daddy's new friend this week?" his mother asked at once.

Bobby, chewing a candy from the bag his grandmother had given him, had to swallow before he could answer. "You know, Mom. The birdbrain."

"Bobby!" His grandmother was sharp. "You shouldn't call anyone a birdbrain. That's not nice, son."

"I know, Gram. Dad said I shouldn't say that but I told him it wasn't me. Mom called Erna a birdbrain. *I* didn't." He licked the chocolate off his fingers.

Muriel gasped. "You told your father I called his girlfriend a birdbrain?" Exasperated, she snapped, "For goodness sakes, Bobby, stop eating all that candy before dinner." She continued to question her son. "What did your father say?"

Bobby paused for a minute. He felt uneasy.

"Well, come on," his mother prodded him. "What did your father say to you?"

He wiped his sticky hands on his trousers and gave his mother his undivided attention. "He said I should tell you that you had a big mouth and that your brains are where you sit. Is that where your brains are, Mom?"

His mother exploded. "How could you be such a tattletale? That's bad!"

Bobby blinked. He looked from his mother to his grandmother.

"But Mom, you did say she was a birdbrain," he protested.

"It's *your* fault." His grandmother pointed her finger at her daughter. "You have no business talking like that to the boy."

Muriel turned on her mother. "You keep out of it!" Then she suddenly burst into tears.

Frightened, Bobby ran to his mother. "Don't cry, Mommy. I won't tell that Erna's a birdbrain anymore. Don't cry. Please!"

Muriel fought back the tear. "It's not your fault, darling. It's mine. Gram's right. I shouldn't have said that about your dad's friend. I promise, I won't say anything like that again."

Bobby hugged her. "Me neither!"

His mother kissed him and tried to smile. "Wash your hands and we'll have dinner." As Bobby left the room Muriel approached her mother. "I don't know what's gotten into me lately. I'm so jumpy and do such dumb things and say such dumb things like calling that Erna names in front of Bobby. I'm sorry, Mother."

The mother put her arms around her daughter. "Don't be too hard on yourself. The hurt is still new. But for Bobby's sake, don't say anything nasty about Don or his friends. Bobby has to be able to love you both."

"You're right, Mom. I know you're right. But it's so hard." And she began to cry again.

Her mother patted her softly. "It takes time," she said. "It takes time."

* * * * * *

The whole condition of divorce creates a long list of unpleasant feelings in most people. Polite men become furious, hostile and ugly about their wives. Pleasant women who are usually meticulous in their rejection of bad behavior resort to absurdity and invectives about their former mates. It generates great anger that infuriates and outrages.

A Texas couple, both psychologists, set out to have a friendly divorce. Each tried valiantly to respect the other until critical words from the father about mother's raising of their only son was relayed by the child after a visit with his father. Soon each was saying nasty things about the other.

"How can you talk that way?" a friend of the couple asked the father. "Just a short time ago you were sharing the same house, eating the same food and using the same towels. Now you describe each other with such hate!"

The father thought for a moment before answering. "I guess it's really difficult to end a marriage without becoming very angry."

Some anger following divorce cannot be avoided and may even be necessary. It helps avoid the depression that most people would otherwise experience. But wholesale anger at an ex-wife or ex-husband creates difficulties for the child.

Don't put your child in the middle of your bad feelings for your former mate. Don't make him a pawn in the sending of messages. He's not on a chess board and shouldn't be used for that purpose. If you're really infuriated with your former spouse, pick up the phone and talk to him or her. If you want to send messages, write them down and let the post office do your talking. You pave the way for all kinds of harm when you use your child as an ambassador of ill will. It requires constant awareness to avoid the use of your children as go-betweens. The price of using them is that it stirs up greater feelings of guilt. They may already be worried that their naughtiness has caused your divorce in some way.

Do not behave like a district attorney and fire questions at the child who returns from a visit with the other parent. If you belittle each other to the child you open the way to self-doubt in your son or daughter. Sometimes one parent will try to poison their child's view of the other parent. This is poisonous to the child as well. The adjustment is hard enough to bear. Don't add to a child's misery by trying to prejudice his feelings and make him lose contact with the other parent. You are no doubt making him feel embarrassed and uncomfortable.

Divorce not only foments bad thoughts, it may even bring about bad behavior. A divorcee in New Hampshire related her complex feelings during the process of separation. She was infuriated by her husband's angry refusal to let her use the family car. Following the argument, she arose at 4 A.M. on a frosty morning, tiptoed into the garage, where she started the car, and deliberately drove it into an ice-covered fire hydrant. There she abandoned the vehicle and spent the rest of the night with a neighbor.

Mischief-making sets a poor example for your kids. You destroy their security and put a stamp of approval on anti-social behavior. In cases of such extreme measures it often takes the attorneys to quiet the participants.

Don't punish your child for telling the truth. If the child comes home from the other parent's house and repeats an unpleasant statement that impugns your motherliness, don't fall upon him and vent the anger you're really feeling about your ex-husband on your child.

The worst thing a parent can do is frequently the easiest and most common reaction. A mother may defend herself out of a sense of guilt. "You kids have no idea what that so-and-so has done to me over the years," or "If it weren't for you kids, I would have left your father years ago."

"This kind of talk should be avoided," explains Dr. Seymour Pastron, psychoanalyst. "Such talk disrupts the child's development by the intrusion of parental guilt. Parents are guilty of dismantling the child's world. Their selfish wishes have taken precedence over the child's needs. This occurs in all families, divorced or not. The parents' selfish wants are in conflict with the needs of the child. This becomes more extreme in divorce or death."

Try not to downgrade the other person. Putting the parent down reflects poorly on you. After all, you were the one who chose him. Your child never made that choice for you. What is to be gained from shaking a child's faith in his father or mother? Your son may reason, if dad's no good, maybe I'm no better.

Of course it's difficult to keep making pleasantries about someone you couldn't live with and to pretend a phoney friendship which you no longer feel, but the fact is you are tied forever to your child's other parent even if you detest each other. You'll always share this child in common despite your true feelings, so it's best to try at the very least for civil politeness toward each other.

Try to accent the positive in the other parent if possible. Say, "Yes, your father's a wonderful swimmer," or "Of course, your father loves you very much too," or "You know, your mom is great at helping you. Yes, she's a terrific cook." Forget what a slob you may think she is. If you're sure he's a lazy bum, don't say so to your child. Try to talk up the good qualities. As one legal wit put it, "If you can't say anything nice, shut up!"

Usually one parent winds up with a greater degree of responsibility to the child than the other. This is always the one with whom the son or daughter lives. The absent parent whom the child no longer sees as frequently may turn into a white knight.

A physician from Buffalo, New York was the product of a divorced home. His father, a wealthy but brutal and unloving man, was sparing in his love as well as financial assistance to everyone in the family, including his son.

Years later, after the father's death, he visited with his father's sisters and brothers in England. To his surprise they heaped adjectives of praise upon his father. They hadn't seen him in years — but his memory had developed an aura of goodness and kindness. They had forgotten that the father had usually overlooked their requests for contact with them. He had developed a white hat through the years of his absence.

Of course it's difficult to hide your true feelings and you may feel that not expressing them is a kind of dishonesty. Try for moderation. Temper your attitudes when discussing the other parent with your child. Employ some degree of diplomacy so that you can avoid family wars. If you belittle a figure as important as a mother or a father to a child you will frighten and confuse him.

A group of divorced people discussing the problem of saying nasty things about the other parent made the following comments.

"I came from a divorced family myself and I can tell you we resented hearing nasty things our parents said about each other even when they were true." This from a woman cashier in Boston.

"I was unrealistic. I tended to defend their daddy too much," said a lab technician in Minnesota.

A Florida dentist expressed himself: "My parents drummed into me as a child, 'If you can't say anything nice, don't say anything at all.' It still seems like good advice."

A mechanic in Michigan admitted, "I was very angry after the divorce and I put my wife and her new husband in a very poor light with the children. I said a lot of nasty things, but so did my ex-wife."

Each parent should try to teach respect for the other.

You're teaching respect for yourself at the same time. What is more important, you're also teaching the child to respect himself.

Explain again that your marital breakup had nothing to do with the children in the family. The problems you had were between the parents. Repeat that you couldn't live together enjoyably any more but emphasize that the mother or father that left did not do so out of any sense of anger or hatred.

People always want to rationalize their behavior but if you're the parent who left home, don't place the blame on the other parent in trying to justify your reasons for leaving. Most children are angry at parents for breaking up their homes. This is hard to accept, but remember it's good for your child to express his anger and to assert his independence of feeling.

Don't tattle. Don't berate. Parents are the models for their children's behavior. Hold up a mirror image for your child that will do you both credit.

If the other parent insists on saying nasty things about you to the child realize that you have to live with it. But don't compound the error by joining that kind of an unpleasant game.

## Part 2    Chapter 6

## Playing One Parent Against the Other

**Some children can be destructively intuitive in a divorce situation. Wanting to bolster their relationship with each parent and thinking to derive the most benefits to their shaky sense of security, they may quickly learn to play off one parent against the other.**

* * * * * *

Sid Turner was thoughtful as he listened to his ex on the phone. Then he held the instrument back from his ear. Her voice was nonstop, shrill as it came over the wires.

"I told you, Jenny!" He tried to be patient. "Todd said you let him go alone and I thought I could let him do it too. Nothing happened to him, so calm down, will you?"

"You're an idiot!" Jenny's voice was an octave higher. "I *never* let him go there alone. He wanted to and I wouldn't let him. He's just playing us against each other and you fell right into it."

She was absolutely right, Sid thought to himself as he replaced the phone on it's cradle. That kid was manipulating them for his own ends. He hated to admit Jenny was right again, but he'd have to watch Todd from now on. Besides, he'd had an inner sense of Todd's secret enjoyment the last time he and Jenny had argued over the phone while Todd was present.

The altercation had centered around a missed dental appointment. Todd had assured his mom that dad said it was O.K. to play ball after school, and anyway, Uncle Harvey never minded and would fix his teeth later on.

Sid's brother had stormed about the missed appointment, reminding him that time was money with a professional man and and that Jenny couldn't bring Todd in to see him at will.

Sid and Jenny had had a real wingding over that one. The decibels of their conversation had almost shattered the phone. Todd listened while they argued and seemed to enjoy the darts he whizzed against the opposite wall.

When he picked Todd up for tennis the following Saturday afternoon, Sid was determined not to be manipulated by his son. They had a real workout on the courts. The little creep's getting really good, Sid thought pridefully as Todd's well-placed serve bounced out of the father's reach.

It was a great set. Sid put his arm around his son's shoulder as they walked off the court. "Whee! You're dripping wet! Me too. Let's get home. A shower will do it." He grinned at his 12-year-old.

"I'll be dry as soon as I cool off for a minute." His son wiped his forehead with his arm. "I don't need to shower. Mom never makes me take one. She knows I'm more comfortable without it and you know good old Mom, she always wants me to be happy."

Sid felt a twinge. Jenny knew just how to make the kid happy. But he caught himself before his thoughts carried him any further.

He stopped, looked at his boy and answered in a way that would have done Dr. Spock credit. He was firm but friendly. "Great try at wheedling your old man to have it your way, but we're heading for home and a shower, good buddy. We're going to get de-smelled, you and me both. Your Mom will be proud of your new fragrance tonight. I'm sure she'll agree with me when we discuss it later, but even if she doesn't, that's how we do it at this end. O.K.?" He boxed his son playfully.

Todd kicked a pebble with his foot and observed his father from under his eyelids. He could see the resolution on his face. "Sure, O.K.," he grumbled at first as they walked toward home and a shower. And then he returned his father's smile.

* * * * * *

A divorced mother whose child plays her against her ex-husband is likely to concur with recent findings that show women without children to be happiest of all. Some angry children learn to manipulate one parent against the other after divorce. They sense the competition of the situation and become adroit in setting one parent against the other to serve what they perceive as their own gain.

The relationship of children with their divorced parents differs widely. As the whole family gropes for adjustment to this new situation, some children will understand that their parents are trying to score brownie points with them and they realize how simple it is to manipulate them. Some parents cooperate in hopes of winning the child over and becoming his favorite. Often their child finds himself in the position of gaining favors first from the one parent and then from the other.

"Sometimes it's just great," a teenager from Los Angeles described his situation. "When I have trouble with Mom, I get Dad to straighten it out for me, and when I have a problem with Dad, I go to Mom. So I usually get my own way about most anything."

Divorce creates emotional havoc and change in the same way as death. When death occurs it has to be accepted as being permanent. When a divorce happens, there is a fear that it is permanent.

"In the process of adapting to the change of permanent or feared permanence," comments psychoanalyst Dr. Seymour Pastron, "one can grow or one can become neurotic, depending on the strength of character that a given child can develop to confront unpleasant change."

A child that tries to manipulate his parents may be angry, insecure or even feel unwanted. It gives him a false sense of power that he may carry over in his dealing with his peers and other adults, and he may use it as a model for future behavior. It develops an unrealistic set of values so that a child may begin to feel it is advantageous to be cunning or to distort the truth. He may also develop the value that "any method that gets him what he wants is O.K.!"

A child who wants more attention may say to his mother, "Dad plays with me all the time but he doesn't think you do." This may be a distortion of what dad actually said or it may even be wholly fabricated. In either case, it's unproductive for the child.

Sometimes the problem of trying to play parents off against each other may stem from two different life styles, and that creates unfamiliarity with the other one's habits. Some children try to capitalize on such situations.

"I like to watch crime stories on T.V. Dad lets me, so why can't I do it here?"

"I don't want to wear my hat outside. Mom says I don't need it."

"Do I have to change my underwear every day? Dad says every other day is enough."

"Gee, you only gave me a dime for after school. Mom gives me a quarter."

Or to a grandmother, "My other grandma gives me money every time I see her."

Parents are people, too, and they frequently can't help but feel competitive with the opposite member who outdoes them or outgives them.

One newly wed couple cited in-law competition as the basis for their best set of china. Every time *his* parents gifted them with a place setting of their pattern, *her* parents would go out and get them a place setting too.

If you sense that your child is setting you off against each other, try not to get involved in that kind of competition. Do what's best for your child and don't become a party to destructive trading. Don't, for instance, become angry because your former husband and son went bowling and didn't fulfill a promise to cut the kid's hair. When you son comes home and says, "It's not my fault, Dad *made* me go bowling." Don't fall into the trap and search for a way to even up the score. If you really have a gripe, deal directly with the other parent. Don't do it through the child.

Sometimes children will pit one parent against the other by trying to enlist their sympathies. "Please, Mom, I get so bored at Dad's house. He never takes me anywhere, so please, please, can't we go to the movies now?"

Beware of a child who may even reward the parent with a gratifying assertion that he loves him or her the best: "We *can* go to the movies? Oh Mom. You're the best. I love you more than I love Daddy. You're better to me than he is."

Take it with a grain of salt, and try to understand some of the motivation behind your child's sudden burst of comparative love.

Don't be overprotective of your child if you and the other parent discover you are being wheedled beyond an acceptable state of wheedledom. Don't challenge an ex-wife who complains that your son couldn't eat dinner after his visit with you. "Of course he's always trying to get me to give him a hot dog. You never bother to get it for him even though you know how much he loves hot dogs! So, I got one for him. He wanted it." Such devices may make your child feel especially deserving or especially guilty. If you're constantly intervening on behalf of your child, you may even create in him feelings of self-doubt and make him feel he is unable to deal with his own problems.

In your reaction to being pitted against the other parent, don't become self-serving and make a companion or a confident out of your kid. It undercuts your position of authority. You can't act like a buddy one minute and revert to being a parent the next.

Parents have to try to be evenhanded in relating to a child who is manipulatory. Sometimes these children will enjoy the chaotic results between his parents. He can feel a false sense of power if a serious argument ensues as a result of his machinations.

There have been situations where a child will *get even* by repeating entire conversations to one parent that the other parent would have preferred left unsaid. If such is the case, try not to involve your child, but be more circumspect the next time, and don't put yourself in a position of vulnerability.

Your child may stir up a hornet's nest because he is frightened. If he's stretching the truth in pitting you against your ex-husband, tell him you know it's not quite that way. Let him know that you disapprove but don't put him down or belittle him. He has to have a good opinion of himself if he is to survive, but that is not to say that he must be always right. He's a child.

Tell him that you understand his wheedling but that you do not like it. Tell him that if he is angry he can kick his football around, or make up a batch of dough and let him punch that around for awhile.

You must assert your disapproval or it may have the opposite effect of seeming to concur with his behavior.

Some parents feel guilty at having inflicted divorce upon their children so they will accept being manipulated by their children as just punishment.

Don't squelch such a child entirely and leave him with no outlets for the insecurity that made him try to "handle" his parents. The bad feelings won't go away. They will only be repressed.

You can't expect your child to be a model of virtue at all times. In the extreme, repression can result in violent antisocial behavior. In less extreme situations, it's the road to ulcers and colitis.

Some schools are beginning to offer courses to children so

they can understand the problems that are created by divorce. Education can be a very helpful tool in zeroing in on the emotional confusion developed by separation and divorce.

Try to find a middle course when you are dealing with a kid who is uneasy about his relationship with his parents and is trying to play them against each other. Don't let him manipulate you. Be loving. Don't waffle on the issues but be kind, constructive and firm.

It is frightening for a child to be in control. No matter how a child may react, he feels much more secure having the parents control him. Parents should strive to be rational, loving authorities, divorced or not.

Your child wants to love both his parents and be loved in return, but most children want to have parents who are understanding and use good judgement. Stay in the driver's seat. Your child understands and wants guiding, responsible parents. First and foremost, a parent should be a parent!

# Part 2 Chapter 7
# Lowered Financial Standards

Many families, torn apart by the emotional effort of living together, are relieved at the prospect of finding personal peace through divorce. Frequently, they do not take into account the difficulties of reduced finances and the problems that this can cause.

* * * * * *

Harriet Jensen tried to dry her eyes before she let her sister through the back door. But Alice noted her puffed face at once.

"Is it Fred? Has he been here bothering you?" Her sister shook her head and resumed weeping.

"Tell me. What's wrong?" Alice was insistent.

Harriet clasped her hands and then pointed to the papers covered with columns of figures on the kitchen table. She tried to answer.

"It's horrible. I just can't manage." Then she plopped down into the kitchen chair and her whole body sagged in despair. "Alice," she said choking back the tears, "I don't know which was worse, my life with Fred or trying to feed my kids without money. I haven't got a cent left. Not a single penny." She let her head drop down between her knees.

"Come on. Let me have a look," her sister pulled the sheaf of papers toward her end of the table and studied them.

But before she could get very far, Colt, aged 6, and his 4-year-old sister, Heather, came barging through the door, banging the screen behind them. They ran to Alice. "Aunt Alice!" They kissed and hugged her.

Then turning to their mother Colt asked, "Mom, can we have 50 cents? All the kids are going to make this thing tomorrow and we each have to put up our share. It's going to be neat, Mom."

"Can we have it? Please, Mom," Heather pleaded.

Once more Harriet burst into tears. "I haven't got it. Don't you kids understand? I have no money," she shouted through the sobs.

Frightened, the children backed off. Harriet, reaching into her purse, pressed two quarters into Colt's hand. He and his

99

sister looked doubtfully at their mother.

"Take it. It's alright," Alice coaxed them. "Go along now. I want to talk to your mom."

An hour later Alice was still pouring over Harriet's budget. "It's really not enough," she said.

Harriet sighed, "It's not fair. Fred has more than half of his usual income just for himself. I have less than half for the three of us. Last month when I tried to work part time in the supermarket, Fred heard about it and sent me less money. After they took out the withholding and stuff, I had less than before, so I quit. What can I do, Alice? Tell me what I can do?" She pleaded with her older sister.

Alice was grim. "For one thing, we're going down to the welfare office on Monday morning. I'm going with you."

"Welfare!" Harriet was stung. "We've never been on welfare."

"Well you never needed it before. You need it now." She was firm. "And then we're going to see the social worker and talk to her about getting you trained for something so you can get a job that pays a fairly decent salary."

She paused before going on. "And for right now, you and the kids are coming over to my house. I've got a big turkey in the oven for dinner." She nudged her sister toward the door. "Come on," she said. "Let's go find the kids. We'll work on this problem one step at a time.

"One step at a time," Harriet repeated after her sister as they closed the door.

* * * * * *

It's difficult to deal with the financial problems that frequently arise after divorce. As a social phenomonon of our times, divorce is expensive. The problem arises because one income that formerly covered the maintenance of one house or apartment, purchased clothes, paid for the food bills, electricity, insurance, car repair, ad infinitum is stretched after divorce to cover two dwelling places, two sets of gas bills, two bills for electricity, food for two tables, etc.... "Well, we were all eating anyway," a father may say, "so what difference does it make?" Any homemaker can explain that four people who eat together can eat for less money than the cost of feeding two pairs of people when each pair purchases their own food of the same kind and quantity. A larger amount of money is needed for the same number of people divided between two households than was necessary when they were all in one group.

Unfortunately, instead of having more money, most people have less. Anyone not fully aware of an oncoming reduced income after divorce can be very troubled indeed.

Let us examine a hypothetical family with a total income of $15,000 per year. After the divorce settlement our family's income is divided so that the father now has $8,200 per year, and the mother and two or three children receive $6,800 in alimony ever year. The husband keeps the money that is left after payment for his sole use. The mother, on the other hand, must support herself and her children on this substantially reduced income. Both are now in a bad fix, but obviously it's far worse for the mother.

This kind of a split in a family income is a fairly good one because most often the mother does not have that large a share of the father's money alloted to her for alimony and child support.

No-fault divorce, with it's desirable aspects, can cause problems for someone angling for increased child support before agreeing to divorce. The husband simply obtains a divorce and the wife is stuck with the settlement, like it or not.

Almost one in four divorcees work. Today it is a necessity. Some who seek divorce are not awarded any alimony or child support, depending upon individual circumstances.

Low-income families often can't afford a legal divorce. They simply separate and the mother, most often left with the children, is forced to seek help from a public aid organization. It is almost pointless for the courts to try to make the father support the mother and children because it's a virtual impossibility for someone with a meager income to divide it up any further. Even middle income families who divorce can barely manage to keep two homes going on the same income, and most often cannot do so.

Some people feel the women's liberation movement has not always worked out to the best monetary interests of divorcing females. Many courts suggest that if women have a sincere desire for equality, then there's no need to shield them from the financial problems of divorce and it is only fair that they should get a job to supplement a reduced income and make out as best they can. Others claim this attitude may stem from the fact that the decision makers in the courts are often men.

Settlements frequently work out to be a round robin of confusion. With only half an income to start with, a women will often supplement this amount of money by working. A husband, hearing that his wife is now working, will then reduce the amount of his subsidy. If the wife then stops working she must apply for public help to keep going. Since this is even more minimal, she may once again seek to work so that she can increase the family income. But public aid will no longer continue if the mother's income increases beyond certain specified amounts. So it is then discontinued. If it weren't all so serious, this sort of financial adadgio dance might almost seem laughable.

The problems in the divorce courts are manifold. Dishonesty on the parts of husbands unwilling to share their incomes is a frequent charge made by wives who are unable to substantiate their suspicions.

One wealthy Wisconsin man whose family owned a trucking firm had an approximate income of $100,000 per year. When he and his wife decided to divorce she never envisioned financial difficulties. The trucking executive, however, managed to have himself placed on the payroll of the family firm as a $17,000 employee although the wife had always believed him to have been a part owner. With the assistance of his father and brother, with whom he did in fact own the business, he was able to secrete a large part of his investments and assets. After the divorce suit was settled the wife was awarded $7,000 a year for herself and their three children. When later she became seriously ill, she was unable to pay for private medical care and had to apply for welfare assistance. Here was a father, more than able to support an ex-wife and his three children, who left them to the care of government agencies. What little he gave to his family was offered as though it were a charitable donation but in a far meaner spirit.

The perplexities don't only confound wives. Many men, having to share a modest income, live bitterly after divorce. They are lonely, miss their children and have to live with the increased demands of alimony and visitations to their children.

Sometimes it is the wife who ends the marriage with most of the combined assets.

An Arizona man who shared an insurance business with his wife refused to send their 19-year-old son back to college after their divorce. The mother, who had always doted on their son, insisted that the father support him through the university, but the father, feeling that the son was not serious in his desires to study, refused to continue payment for any further schooling. The wife was furious but the father felt justified. His ex-wife, he explained, was not only receiving alimony from him, but had a previous inheritance that she had kept intact after the divorce settlement. She also maintained her share in their insurance business. "She's got much more money than I have," declared the insurance man. "If she wants to let that slob play around in college on her money, she can do it. I'm not giving him any more of mine!"

In the main, most divorce settlements award smaller incomes to women. Husbands usually retain the larger share of their earnings. Those wives seeking to end a marriage should be aware that they will have to care for their children almost single handed and that the greater part of the financial burden will fall on them.

No matter what the decision of the courts may be, a large number of fathers never live up to all of their alimony and child support agreements. If they are brought to court and fined heavily, they may not be able to pay it, and if they are put in jail for non-payment they certainly can't pay.

Anyone involved in a divorce action should have their lawyer spell out property division, visitation, alimony, medical insurance for the parents and children, custody, etc. Spelling it out may help minimize the problems that occur later.

Formerly, obtaining credit ratings after divorce was a problem for women, but the Federal Equal Credit Opportunity Act now prohibits discrimination because of marital status. Any divorced person who has the capability to enter into a binding contract cannot be denied credit. No longer is a spouse restricted from sharing in the former mate's credit history.

Divorce often created prejudicial opinions against the participants. A recent national television newscast reported a confidential insurance company memo that indicated that those who had separated or divorced in the past year were considered to be a poor risk.

Divorce litigations record endless accusations by all parties concerned, with right and wrong on all sides. Much of it revolves around financial divisions. Money often exhibits peculiar properties. It can be an expression of love when it is given away, it can be used to purchase material things or it can be used to purchase material things that are offered as signs of affection. It can also be withheld as a punitive device. But good or bad, it's one of the prime bones of contention during divorce and is one of the most frequent subjects for debate.

If you are seeking to divorce, be sure that you are well represented with legal counsel and that all your needs are as well met as they can be under your particular set of circumstances.

## Part 2 Chapter 8

## If It's Your Child's Day With the Other Parent and He Doesn't Show Up

A child whose parent has promised to spend time with him, and reneges on that promise without reason, causes anguish and heartbreak to that child. If they do not understand the missed appointment, boys and girls cannot help but feel that the parent is uncaring and has abandoned them.

* * * * * *

"Hurry up, Mommy," Beverly's daughter prodded her. "Get up It's almost 8:30 already."

Beverly stretched in feigned langor. "It's my only day to sleep. There's no hurry. Your father will probably be late. Who knows, he may even be stuck somewhere and won't be able to come at all today." She tried to sound casual.

"No, no. He won't be late." Tammie was emphatic. "Get up, Mommy. Time for breakfast."

She knew her daughter didn't like to discuss her father, but Beverly's heart sank. She recognized Tammie's unswerving faith in Eddie. For years, she herself had been certain that he would do whatever it was that he had promised; until finally she had recognized him for what he was: an unreliable person. How long would it take her daughter, she wondered, to come to the same conclusion. She wished she could forsee a happier future between Tammie and her father.

Beverly stalled getting breakfast but it was no use. By 9 o'clock, the girl was at the living room window, her eyes sweeping the street in anticipation as she swallowed her last bite of toast.

A half hour later Tammie was very anxious. "Maybe something happened. Maybe there was an accident! Can I call his house, Mom?" she asked.

But the call brought no response and Tammie chewed her finger nails.

Beverly, watching her, thought the bum probably never came home last night.

By 10 o'clock, Tammie was a crumpled mass of hurt. The mother ached for her daughter as she slumped into the big lounge chair near the window. Between sobs she wailed, "He promised, he promised."

When the crying subsided a little, Beverly suggested a visit to the zoo, but Tammie showed no interest in the outing. She writhed and punched the black leather chair. She even tried to kick Beverly. The mother caught her daughter's leg and held it firmly for a moment. Then she cuddled her daughter and comforted her.

"I think Daddy wants to be with you. He really does. He just can't keep a promise. He doesn't keep his promises to anyone."

Her daughter rubbed her eyes. "He's mean."

"No, he's not." Beverly tried to explain. "He's just not reliable. That's the way he is." Then changing the subject, she suggested, "I've got a great idea. We'll call Aunt Ann and Geraldine and we'll all go down to the Grand and see the new movie. How about it?" She pulled her daughter up out of the chair and straightened her clothes.

Beverly was determined to help dull her child's disappointment in her father. As they left the house Tammie was finally regaining some interest in their plans.

"Can we have a pizza for dinner?" she asked.

Beverly sighed. "Of course, darling. That's a delicious idea.

* * * * * *

All parents are not able to keep the promises they make, but it is irresponsible to feel it is unimportant to abide by a date that a mother or father has made to visit with a child. Making plans with children are just as vital as any commitment to adults. A parent who cannot keep to pre-arranged plans should let the child know of his changed intentions. It is sad for a boy or girl to have a parent who doesn't explain and doesn't show up. Not only is the actual promise of concern but it jeopardizes the child's sense of self-esteem and the relationship with that parent.

How well the absent parent and a child get along affects the at-home parent also. If your child returns from a visit with the father or mother who live elsewhere and is upset or overstimulated, you have to cope with the aftereffects of his behavior. It may be far worse, if the child sits expectantly waiting for a parent who does not arrive. The one at home must deal with the child's emotional turmoil and the blow to his ego.

If a son or daughter complains, "He doesn't love me. If he loved me he wouldn't forget all about me," how does one convince a child it's not so? The parent knows it is important for the son or daughter to feel loved so he or she can be loving, but you, the parent, may think the father or mother behaves like a bum and a ne'er-do-well yourself.

Perhaps this was a contributing factor to your divorce. The other parent may always have been unreliable but now your own feelings must be set aside so that you can buffer your child's acute disappointment. You may want to hurl invectives or make excuses, yet for your child's sake you should try to offer a calm plausible explanation.

Under the best of circumstances the mother or father who has custody of the children must ready them to go visiting. The parent gets the kids cleaned up and waits with them for the ex-spouse to arrive and cart them off. If you are the at-home parent, you are left to your own devices. Even if you have personal plans there is a sense of being left out of this portion of your children's lives. The father and the children form a little family unit from which you know you are excluded. The father, no doubt, feels the same about the family circle you create with the children. With the exception of graduations, weddings, etc., the two units are not likely to overlap.

When your kids return from their visit they may be depressed or excited. You are on the outside of that experience but you have to listen to the chatter or look at the long faces and go on with your parental chores; washing their hair, putting them to bed, checking homework and many other such responsibilities. The other parent has dropped the children off at your door and sailed away to a carefree life.

Under the worst of circumstances you get your child ready. You both wait and the expected parent is a no-show. You then have to deal with all the emotional rejection your child feels at such a time. You have to substitute some other activity to take the place of the hoped-for visit, and you have to salvage your child's feelings so he will not be utterly smashed by his disappointment.

You even have to stumble around and try to explain the missed appointment. You can't come right out and tell your kid his father is no good, if that's what you think. No matter how irritated or upset the incident has made you, too, it's demoralizing for your child if you bad mouth his other parent. What you say must be said tactfully so it won't reflect on your child.

His security is threatened by a parent who has promised to share time and then does not live up to the commitment. How does he know you won't do this to him too? He may reason that one day you too will not be there to care for him, either. Such anxieties may seem well grounded to a rejected boy or girl. And the results can create tremendous fear and insecurity.

Why do some parents continue to offer love and devotion to children of divorce while others disapper into the mist? There may be a variety of reasons. Some absent parents back out of their children's lives after divorce because they find the memories too painful to bear. They are unable to handle the situation to such a degree that they simply walk away from it.

One San Diego father tried at first to see his children on a regular basis. After each visit he found himself weeping and feeling so hopeless that ultimately he stopped seeing his children at all. He could not cope with the situation at any level.

There may be bad feelings between the mother and father. Sometimes the father hates the mother so much that he cannot bear to be anywhere near her and gives up the children so he can avoid contact with the former wife.

Or there can be such negative influence by a mother who constantly berates her ex-spouse to their children, that she poisons the atmosphere and turns the children against that parent. The visits become so strained and unpleasant that they soon die off, much to everyone's relief. It is sad when a mother's control of her aggression and anger is so defective that it harms the children and creates this kind of a loss for them.

On occasion, illness makes it impossible for a divorced person to continue parenting. Mental illness or physical impairment may destroy a relationship. Alcoholism, too, separates many parents from their sons and daughters.

A San Francisco woman related her relief when the father stopped visiting their son. When the father was drunk he would beat the boy during visits. Each time he took the son away, the mother worried. The child was taken to taverns, left alone and misused. At last, court intervention terminated the father's right to visit.

A Massachusetts father with a serious psychosis was unable to accept the responsibility of parenthood when he was hospitalized. A parent's emotional disturbance places a heavy burden on children. There are, however, many incidents of divorced parents with chronic mental illness who raise children or visit successfully during periods of remission.

"Children can identify with positive aspects even in unstable parents," says child psychoanalyst Dr. Seymour W. Friedman.

If a parent has a debilitating physical illness, it may prevent contact with their children of divorce. Sometimes parents are even ashamed or hurt by a child's reaction. A South Carolina mother related how her ex-husband left off his visits with their daughter after his face was scarred in a fire. From that point on their 3-year-old daughter never saw her father again.

It is very sad when a mother won't permit a child to see a father because she is punishing the other parent, or vice versa. She is, in effect, punishing her child and denying him the comfort of contact with the other parent.

No matter how seldom a child may see the other parent following divorce, contact with each other is important. Where the relationship is pleasant, a child thinks fondly of his parent. If the relationship has been unpleasant, the child may have a peculiar view or the absent parent and his recall will be hazy. If an absent parent has dropped a relationship with a child and shows no signs of wanting to resume contact, it is best for a child to try to accept the situation as it really is.

Writing to syndicated columnist Ann Landers, a teenager describes her attempts to contact an absent parent. The following is the letter and Miss Lander's astute reply.

*Dear Ann Landers,**

*My parents were divorced when I was ten.*

*I'll be 16 soon and have not seen my father for four years although he has visiting rights. I think about him a lot.*

*Just before Christmas I asked my teacher if I should write him a letter telling him about my interests. She said, "Yes,*

---

* Reprinted with the permission of Ann Landers: Field Newspaper Syndicate and the Chicago Sun-Times.

but don't let your mother know."
I wrote a long letter and sent a small picture of myself. I haven't received an answer. Should I write again and ask if my letter got lost in the Christmas rush?

Hopeful

Dear H:
Your teacher gave you bad advice. If you know where your dad is, he knows where you are. Let him be.

It's not hard to build fantasies around a daddy who isn't there. Don't let your imagination trick you into thinking he is something he is not, honey.

It is really difficult for a youngster who longs to have contact with a formerly seen parent. He feels hurt if the father or mother no longer visits with him. If he also assumes it is his fault, brought about by his anger with the parent at a former time, he may feel increasing guilt. There are so many occasions during the process of growing up when children need to be supported by the contact with parents: school activities, plays, scout outings, go-to-school night, religious occasions, etc. When they must attend to these needs without parental bolstering, kids may feel very envious of other children.

It creates solo decisions for the at-home parent. It there's no other parent to consult with, you can't ask, "Should we put braces on him this month or wait a few weeks?" "Is it alright if he spends spring vacation in Florida with his grandmother?"

Frequently there is concern that a child without the other parent will become the unhealthy focal point of the remaining parent's life. This child may wind up as a mama's boy or girl if the mother or father becomes overly dependent on her, or the child may revolt and withdraw from the parent at the earliest opportunity.

During early life, a child develops basic attitudes of trust through the attentions that the mother pays to him. As he or she grows older, he flirts with independence and turns towards the development of his own life. A parent who can't let go stiffles such growth.

A Chicago man was so fearful as he observed his child's developing independence that he nailed wooden bars to the apartment windows on the pretext that he worried about the child falling from their second floor. "I used to want to ask him if the bars weren't there because he had an unconscious desire to throw our son out the window," the mother explained after their divorce.

Some psychologists feel that income plays a part in the degree of contact between parent and child following a divorce. Those with low incomes tend to abandon their children more readily than do those fathers who earn more money. A low-income parent may not see his child ever again but the parent who earns more money will usually see his child at least a few times a year.

Adolescent relationships with parents are different from those a parent shares with his younger children. During this period of a son or daughter's life, they tend to strike out on their own and may not want to tag along with dad. Many teenagers dislike family outings at this time. They often prefer peer relationships and would much rather be with their own social circles than to be bored with parental choices.

A divorced father, sensing such rejection, may misinterpret the reasons as relating solely to himself. If the parent is sensitive, he will stop trying to visit and develop a "I won't call you until you call me," kind of attitude. If he suggested an outing and his son or daughter chose a club meeting over spending time with him, he may be hurt. Sometime the father stops coming and then the child, eventually aware of his father's absence, also becomes hurt at his dad's coolness toward him. Confusion and misunderstanding can result in a permanent loss of contact between father and teenage children.

Younger children who feel abandoned and unloved by a parent can become seriously depressed.

It is apparent that children need both parents and when they lose contact with the mother or father they must make a difficult adjustment to life with a single parent. The age, background and emotional reserve of the individual will have a great deal to do with the kind of adjustment the child is able to make.

What should you do if you've gotten your child ready for a visit with the other parent and he doesn't show up? Try, first of all, to remain reasonable. Attempt to be honest and truthful and to keep the lines of communication open. Listen to your child as sincerely as you can. The more he can express his disappointment, the easier it will be for him to bear.

Don't attack the other parent. You, as the remaining parent, have to carry on both roles. Some people reason that if the remaining parent is deeply committed to the child he will not feel the absence of the other parent as keenly.

"Children have a great deal of trouble dealing with rage at the parents who have put them in this dilemma," say Dr. Martha Kirkpatrick, psychiatrist at the University of Southern California. "The parents should maintain some kind of communication with each other. Hopefully the child can learn that parental care has not been divorced from his life."

Try to explain to children that they should not expect too much if you know the other parent will be lax in his commitment to the child. Tell your child that his father is not the kind of person who can live up to his promises, but it does not mean that he doesn't love his child. Be sure to emphasize that *you* love your child very, very much.

Try to get your child to talk it out. He will probably feel depressed and angry. "Why me?" he'll say. Or "How come Susie's father doesn't do that?" A child will get over the hurt much faster if he or she can ask questions freely of you without worrying that you will be angered by what is said.

Assure your child that the two of you will always have a loving, caring relationship and that he can always depend on you. If your attitude oozes certainty some of this is going to rub off on him and make him feel much more secure.

If your child is crushed by the lack of attention of the other parent, take your child away and try to distract him. Don't get angry and attack the other parent. This will only hurt your child too. Protect the image of the other parent so your child can still feel some warmth and love for him.

Reassure him that his father does love him but has an adult problem. Above all try to let your child retain a sense of his own worth and do everything you can to help him in this regard.

## Part 2  Chapter 9

## How Do You Provide Your Child With Adult Companionship if the Other Parent Doesn't Come Around Anymore?

Do children who are missing one parent as the result of a divorce situation have to substitute someone of the same sex with whom they can identify? Do they need a surrogate to fill that void? If an out-of-house parent stops visiting, some children wonder why they can't have two parents, like most children. Such worries can cause them anguish and unhappy reactions.

* * * * * *

Dear Sue,

    I can't tell you how much I appreciated your invitation to take Cindy and Pam for the month of August. Kelly is going up to the boy's camp with Mr. Donovan, his club leader, and the other boys in his group. He'll have a wonderful month too. He is absolutely crazy about Mr. Donovan. It's been a blessing. It's like he's his second father. He was so depressed after Tom stopped seeing the children. Now he's a changed boy again. After Tom left I didn't know where to turn or what to do with the kids. Finally I got a job but it was tough on Kelly. He was 11 you know, and quite capable. He had to take care of the girls before and after school when I was at work. My job was in a bakery, nine to five, but I had to leave before the kids had breakfast and I didn't get home until 6 P.M. Kelly had to drop out of all of his after school activities and he was so unhappy over the divorce. All the kids missed their father. But Kelly adored him and Tom hadn't even had the decency to send the kids a postcard.

    Anyway, it was almost a year before I realized that Kelly seemed peculiar. He was in a world of his own and so unhappy. It scared the daylights out of me.

My neighbor's sister is a social worker and she recommended the agency I went to. That was the best thing I could have done for myself and the three kids. They helped me get a factory job on the night shift. Now I get home at 7:30 A.M. in time to make breakfast and get the kids off to school. All three of them eat lunch at school and stay for after school activities while I sleep. Then we all have dinner together and I'm home until 10:30 P.M. They're all asleep when I leave them with Kelly so it's not as big a responsibility for him.

Best of all is what happened to Kelly. He rejoined the boy's club and has become very friendly with Mr. Donovan, the new group leader. In fact, he's crazy about him. He doesn't seem as upset about Tom anymore. It's been a godsend. He's so much happier now that he has someone to substitute for his father.

Anyway, you can imagine how thrilled Kelly was when your invitation arrived for Cindy and Pam. He was dying to go to camp with Mr. Donovan and the boys in the club and now he'll be able to go for the whole month while the girls are visiting with you.

You're wonderful for being so thoughtful.

I'll call in a few days and tell you what time Cindy and Pam will arrive.

                       All my love and gratitude,
                       Edith

\* \* \* \* \* \*

One of the important aspects of growing up with a mother and father is that each one serves as a male and female role-model for their children. Boys and girls learn role expectations from both parents. If one parent absents himself children must model themselves on someone else who is the same sex as the missing parent.

Writing about the need for parent substitutions in their book *Growing Up Healthy*, pediatrician Dr. Diego Redondo and Edith Freund answer a divorced mother who worries about proper parental care for her baby. "Your daughter should have the acquaintance of a father figure in her life," Dr. Redondo and Edith Freund advise. "This could be her grandfather, her uncle or a family friend. She needs to know what men and women are like and that there are dependable adults around her."

Raising a masculine child without a father and having no one to serve as a model for his maleness creates the possibility of homosexual orientation. It is one of the parental concerns of raising a male child in a mother-only home. A son may not look to his father as a life model if he is overly close and intimate with his mother, and has a feeling of anger or hostility toward the father he seldom or never sees.

Such fears are not always justified, since homosexuality seems to occur just as frequently in a home that contains a mother as well as a father. But there are other factors to consider as well. Authorities agree that a poor relationship with the father and unusually close ties with the mother may serve as predisposing factors that stimulate latent homosexuality in some. Other aspects that may work to develop this condition are an endocrine imbalance or special kinds of physical development.

Girls too may suffer from father-lack in a mother-only home. Adolescent daughters, deprived of a male parent, often strive for masculine attention and approval of men or boys with whom they come in contact.

The problems are not all centered in mother-only homes. Fathers who raise children without a mother also have to deal with adverse reactions that may set in with the absence of a female figure in the home.

The greater concern is for boys since on a whole they seem more vulnerable to stress than girls. They have more than double the number of emotional problems than girls have.

"At every age, boys have greater morbidity and mortality than girls," says psychoanalyst Dr. Martha Kirkpatrick. Contrary to the usual image of the big, strong male, scientific data give us an opposite picture. It is the fragile girl who seems to have more resistance to the emotional and physical strains of life. "Perhaps it is a male dominated culture that has perpetuated the idea of a stronger male figure," Dr. Kirkpatrick adds.

Most perplexing of all is the fact that no one can explain why males are more vulnerable. As yet there have been no answers to this complex riddle. But because of their greater inclination to become troubled there is more concern for the boy who is left without a father than for a girl who is in the same situation.

What happens if a mother is a clinging vine and envelops her son during his years of growing? For one, it interferes with his development.

A son related how disturbing it was for him when his mother used to dress, undress and bathe, in his presence. When a relative suggested the inadvisability of her behavior, her reply was, "We're related. We're family. What difference does it make?" The mother was unaware that her behavior contained the possible seeds of danger to her son.

The son was born to this immigrant mother's second marriage. She remarried without having divorced the first husband who remained in the country where she had formerly lived. Her second husband, a pious man, discovered her indiscretion only after the birth of their child. From then on the marriage was unhappy.

A few years later the father died, leaving the mother to focus on her only son. Disappointed and lonely, she seldom permitted her son to do anything on his own. The mother always prevented him from independent action for fear something would happen to him. Under the guise of motherly love she discouraged him from going on a picnic, going out to play or doing anything without her. Ultimately she even chose his wife.

Such overwhelming attentions discourage a child from developing the ability to make choices on his own. He has a difficult time whether it is selecting a college or going somewhere.

Sometimes called "smother love" because of the nature of the emotional involvement between mother and child, it may possibly conceal deep hostility and cause tremendous guilt in the child who makes some attempt to get away from an overbearing mother.

The parent who overwhelms the child with blanket restriction and is always concerned with imagined or real dangers may be a parent who in reality wishes the child had never been born. Divorced parents who are overanxious may in reality wish they did not have the added burden of raising a child in an already difficult situation.

A child who is deprived of a divorced father or mother faces the possibility of many kinds of unpleasant reactions. If a young child regards the father as some kind of a super figure whom he has offended in some way, he may view his absence as a kind of deserved punishment. Some children reason, "Daddy left because he didn't love me. He didn't love me because I'm not good enough to be loved by anyone." A child who thinks he has been abandoned by a parent feels direct or indirect rage that may be exhibited by withdrawal symptoms, depression or even delinquent behavior.

Once in a while children from intact homes are not permitted to play with children from divorced homes. In such cases the child of divorce may feel he is a defective human being.

Some of today's children without fathers are children of divorce by proxy. The parents are sometimes couples who had been living together without being married. When they decide to "split" each goes his own way and the child is usually left with the mother. There is no legal responsibility to the children so the father often goes off and has no further contact with them.

In general, abandonment may lead a child to be distrustful of other people. Again, his reasoning may be, "My father wasn't trustworthy and other people aren't either. You just can't trust anyone."

How do you find a stand-in for an absent father or mother? As noted earlier other family members can be wonderful models. Aunts, uncles, grandfathers, brothers, friends of the family — all can be excellent substitutes to a small child who is missing a parent in his home.

Teachers, scout leaders, community group leaders . . . all have frequently been fine surrogates for children needing a father (mother) image in their lives. Religious leaders in Sunday schools can also be very helpful if a child relates well to them.

Many organizations, such as Parents Without Partners, throughout many sections of the country have a variety of activities directed at helping divorced people and their children. Some of their groups specifically serve as substitutes for children who need a pattern for an absent parent.

Helpful organizations can be found in phone books under such names as Big Brothers or Big Sisters. Community and religious leaders can be consulted about locating assistance. Counseling services and mental health groups can be investigated. Family doctors, too, may direct patients to organizations that deal with parental absence.

On a personal level a mother who raises her children in a

fatherless home can employ young reliable college men as sitters for her kids. Fathers can have female college students help take care of his young children. A full-time, motherly housekeeper can be a wonderful mother substitute for the father who can afford such a measure.

In a fatherless home, a mother might even consider a college student as a live-in sitter. Sometimes it is possible to have an arrangement where household services and baby sitting are exchanged for room and board.

One Florida divorcee has successfully raised her children with the help of live-in graduate students from a nearby university.

Ideally it would be wonderful to get a parent substitute who would remain with your children while they were growing up. If this is not possible, as it is not in most cases, other kinds of substitutions must be made.

A thoughtful lover who shares your home can also offer role-model companionship for the children of their partners. A succession of lovers however is undesirable and may compound the problems.

Children of divorce don't have to be emotional failures. A good parent protects and provides for his or her child and encourages him to live a full life. Such mothers or fathers are genuinely concerned about the child and try to understand his emotional needs.

An understanding parent of divorce who notices that her child is being overwhelmed by her attentions and anxieties would do well to look for other outlets in her own life and encourage her child to find a father substitute. A good surrogate relationship can reinvest a child with faith and trust and permit his or her constructive development and growth.

## Part 2 Chapter 10
## If You Have to Work

**Often mothers, figuring out the mathematics of separation, soon come to the conclusion that they have to supplement their income by working. Once home most of the time and available, a working mother's child may suddenly find an overwhelming number of changes in his life.**

* * * * * *

It was all over between Esther and Gerald Hopewell. But they were still living under the same roof albeit not in the same room. Gerald had moved into the attic bedroom over the garage where he planned to stay until the lawyers had everything worked out for their separation.

They tried to carry on as though nothing had happened for the sake of their son, Chipper. Although Esther kept mentioning from time to time that soon she would be going to work like daddy did, Chipper, almost 4, seemed only momentarily perplexed. When they told him they were going to be divorced by next fall, he was frightened, but as his life went on in the same manner, it seemed to his parents that he soon got used to the idea that dad was now up over the garage. One night, he had had a bad dream and he had come screaming into Esther's room in the middle of the night crying out, "Mommy! Daddy! Mommy! Daddy! I want my Mommy and Daddy." Gerald came rushing down the narrow hall, wrestling one arm into his robe, his eyes only half open and his sandy hair tousled to one side where he had slept on it. He reached out to help cradle their son who by now nestled in his mother's arms. Momentarily, all three were wrapped around each other. The boy reached out for both of them and clung there, not wanting to let go of either one. After they had calmed him down, Esther had gently placed the boy into Gerald's arms and together they had tucked him securely into his bed.

"I guess there's no way for a kid not to feel his parent's separation," Esther murmured as they withdrew from Chipper's room and each turned to go their separate ways to their own rooms. Gerald sneered under his breath and mumbled something unrecognizable to Esther.

The next morning Esther caught Gerald standing at the refrigerator door downing a glass of juice before leaving for his office.

"We've got to talk," she said.

"Not now. I'm late," Gerald growled.

Esther shrugged. This is the way it always was. Why should it be different now, she thought. I'll just have to make as many of the arrangements as I can without his help.

An hour later she was on the phone with her mother.

"Will you help me, Mom? If you'll stay with Chipper while I take a refresher course in shorthand, I may be able to start a job before we have to sell the house and move. I think that will be so much easier on Chipper, don't you?" She paused, sighing with relief as she listened to her mother's reply.

She summed up her mother's suggestions. "So you think we should visit the day care center a few times so Chip can make friends with the teacher?" That sounds like a good idea." She paused only a moment before she continued. "And the kids too. He'll get to know some of the kids before I start him there. I think you're absolutely right, Mom."

As she hung up she sighed again. How lucky she was to have her mother. And if she introduced Chipper to their new life gradually, it would be so much easier. She was already planning to fill Chipper's new bedroom, wherever it would be, with as many of his old familiar toys as possible. By the time they moved he would be used to the idea of having her at work so that everything wouldn't be happening to him all at one time.

Now if she could only get Gerald to listen so they could work out the details. Unconsciously, she crossed her fingers as she looked for the phone directory so she could find the name of the secretarial school.

* * * * * *

After a hard look at their alimony, child support allowance, insurance or social security benefits, many divorced women head for the work force to supplement what funds they have and support their own new lifestyles and those of their children.

To the older mother who has little or no training for any specific job outside of housekeeping, the prospect may be terrifying and demeaning. The same holds true of a divorcee who married too young to acquire any specialized professional skills. Before entering into the job market, it is often necessary for these women to enroll in various learning programs. On occasion they may find employment where they have on the job training.

Not too many years ago society looked down it's collective nose at a woman who married and went out to work to supplement her husband's income. The hangover from Victorianism decreed that the "little woman" should be dainty and helpless. Even the pre-World War II debutante frittered her days away in meaningless activities. But the present day lifestyle has made the idea of working more and more popular. The employment rate of mothers with young children who work has more than doubled since the end of the second world war.

Numerous factors have contributed to the increased number of female workers: higher education, fewer children and a continuing lineup of helpful housekeeping devices that would boggle the mind of anyone who kept house a mere 50 years ago. Microwave cooking, electric floor scrubbers and buffers, home freezers, advanced washing and drying equipment, non-iron clothing and variety after variety of prepared foods in the supermarkets are all available now to assist the working mother.

The rise in divorce rates has added considerably to the numbers of women wanting or having to work.

Marian B., a divorcee from Tennessee, took to the only specialty she knew. Raised in a small town, she moved to a larger city, enrolled her four children in the local school and was soon much in demand as a domestic day worker.

Debbie H., finding herself divorced and responsible for two children, returned to school with the cooperation of her ex-husband and finished an advanced degree in speech therapy. Armed with her new professional standing, she soon found employment with a local school and was able to develop a small private practice in addition to her full-time job. She plans never to give up her employment even if she should remarry.

There are additional monetary needs for the newly divorced working mother. She has to purchase the extra clothes that are required for her job, which in turn create extra cleaning bills. She must have extra funds for carfare, lunch and a very large extra payment for individual or group care for her children. There is no husband to buffer the financial demands.

In addition she has to worry about the adjustment her children have to make to having a working mother. The very fact that she is working, necessary or not, causes a separation from her kids.

If a divorced mother's children are under the age of 3 it is almost critical for her to try to remain at home with them. A small child who is left at home to be tended by someone else may feel uprooted and afloat without his mother. Extreme change is highly traumatic, even for adults. Many older adults fear moving or relocating because they are uncomfortable at the prospect of uprooting themselves.

During the early years, a child develops a self image and a sense of identity that relate to his later capacity to be able to "hang in there" in the face of change. A stable home, his background, the traditions of his family or community all make him feel part of something that goes on and on. For these reasons, it is very important to permit a young child to develop in a secure home environment before he is sent to a day care center or left with a stranger while the mother works.

Unfortunately, money hangs like a cloud over divorce, and with the best of intentions to stay home and rear their children, many divorced mothers soon find that they must go out and find a job.

If you think such will be the case, try to tell your children you'll be working even before the divorce. If you are able to train yourself for a job while you are still living with your husband, do so. It is even preferable to start work while you are still married, but understandably, many women wish to neither work nor train for work before they are divorced for fear it will influence the amount of alimony or child support they may receive in the future.

If you have to put your child into a new setting such as a day care center, try to introduce him to it and let him get acquainted with it before you leave him there.

Tell your child the facts of your proposed employment without burdening him or frightening him. Children who can understand, and especially older children, should be made aware that the parents are splitting the family income two ways and that it will be necessary for you to work so you can all get along. Older children can also seek part-time employment to help the family budget.

If you're working partly to develop a new interest, tell your children. There's nothing wrong with them understanding that you are a human being with needs too.

But be dependable about coming home from work. And be available to your kids when you return. Let your children know you need help in getting dinner, setting things up before you get home, or running the washer or dryer if you have one in your home. There are many areas where children can share with adults in a new set-up.

After dinner, try sitting with your children while they do their homework. Even if you're not talking to each other, it makes for a pleasant time of togetherness if you all sit around the table and you do some small chores while the children study. If a child wants to know how to spell a word or a small joke is exchanged or an incident at school is related, you will develop a spirit of family and being together that is wonderful for a child. You, too, may want to share an incident about your own work.

The manner in which you accept your job will rub off on your kids. If you constantly complain about any job that you have and give the impression that working is undesirable, your children are going to grow up feeling that way too.

If you do have a difficult job, you can tell your children about it and let them know you are doing it partly for them. Don't make them feel guilty because you have to work, but make them aware that it is pleasurable to do things for others too.

No matter what you say, often *how* you say it and the loving attitude you have is far more important to children than what you are actually saying.

Sometimes it's a good idea to let your kids see where you work if that is possible.

If the idea of working scares you and you think you can't take over the role of being head of the household, you may find, to your surprise, that it can be very pleasant after a while to look to yourself for security. You don't have to be half of anything. You can be your own person, a whole one at that.

A word about working fathers whose children live with him. He shares the same problems as the working mother and must provide substitutions for his children. Although his role as a worker is more usual, he still has to provide supervision for the children during his work hours.

If a child is well supervised while the parent works and the parent is really interested in the child when he is at home, the child will grow up secure, happy and able to accept his own adulthood when it happens.

Make sure that your children know they are responsible for letting you know of their whereabouts. Especially with teenagers, it is important for them to know that they are being supervised even if you are not around them all the time.

How your children will react to your being out of the house while you work will depend on a variety of factors, such as their ages, who stays with them when you are away, where you live, other family circumstances, their relationship with their peers and each other.

## Part 2    Chapter 11
## If Your Child Needs Professional Help

**If your child shows signs of being unusually disturbed by the dissolution of your marriage and does not seem to be getting over it, you may need to consult a professional about his (her) behavior. Divorce is a highly stressful condition to parents and to children alike.**

\* \* \* \* \* \*

Jane sighed as she read the note from the principal that Bard had brought home from school.
Dear Mrs. Hollman:
   I am suspending Bard from further attendance at school. His behavior is more and more anti-social and he seems unreachable. In addition, he has become highly destructive. Today he threw a heavy book at the child in front of him. It was fortunate that she was not hit. Yesterday he smashed a school model made by a team of his classmates.
   I am sorry to report such news but it is now imperative that you come in tomorrow at 10 A.M. for a conference with the school psychologist.
                    Sincerely yours,
                    Wanda Heller, Principal
   Jane's eyes were filled with tears of frustration by the time she had finished the letter. She looked up at Bard, her 7-year-old son, who was working his face into rhythmical contortions and hopping from one leg to the other. He perplexed her.
   "Stand still," his mother ordered him, "and stop making all those funny faces, will you?"
   Bard mumbled something undiscernible.
   "How could you behave so badly in school? Ever since your Dad and I divorced, you've been going from bad to worse. I don't know what's the matter with you." She paused and walked around the kitchen. "Your older sister and brother don't act like you do. Why don't you take an example from them? Answer me!" Then her voice softened. "What's the matter, son. Tell me what's wrong. I know you're miserable. I

want to help you."

Bard mumbled again. "I want to go in my room," he said ignoring his mother's speech.

"What for?" Now his mother was irritated. "Why don't you ever go out and play? All you do is stay in your room." Then, in disgust, she added, "Soon you'll have to stay there all the time because I don't think they're going to let you back in school anymore."

The next morning Jane Hollman kept the appointment at school. She was stunned as she drove home from the conference. Bard was at home, probably still in his room. He was sick. Really sick. The school psychologist had left little doubt of that after their discussion. If she didn't get immediate help for him, he might have to be hospitalized. He might need it, anyway. But he could not return to school until she had obtained some professional help for him.

She knew he was unhappy, but she hadn't known how bad it really was. How had it all happened? And why this child? Her older children didn't seem affected. Was it her divorce or would it have happened anyway?

Like a typewriter, her mind slid from her unanswered questions to the next line of the psychologist's conversation. "If he broke his leg, you would get help for him. This is another type of illness and also requires help. But you can't ignore it anymore than you would a ruptured appendix or pneumonia."

She wouldn't ignore it. She wanted to help Bard in every way she could. He was her baby. She wanted him to get well, and she was grateful for the appointment with the Juvenile Research that the psychologist had made for Bard.

Suddenly she wanted to get home to her son and tell him that soon he wouldn't have to suffer anymore. Help was coming on Monday morning, and Monday wasn't very far away.

* * * * * *

The effects of divorce on children are just beginning to be studied so there is, as yet, no way to know how many children are unable to handle the emotional impact of the destruction of their families. Each child has a different set of defenses, and reactions vary to the stress of divorce. There are areas that an individual may handle well and others where the same child will have difficulties. For example, one child of divorce will continue to do good work in school and have a good relationship with the mother, but can't adjust to getting along with the father. Another child may have a reverse relationship.

Many, many problems may result after the dismantling of a family. Children may become irritable and have temper tantrums. They may become overly possessive of their belongings. They may want to sleep with their mother and worry about being separated from her. They may miss the father acutely and cry or whine.

At any age a child may not sleep well or may not feel like eating. He can be angry, ashamed, have headaches, stomach aches and be terribly depressed. There's no end to the reactions of having a child's world smashed apart.

There doesn't seem to be any *good* time to divorce but there have been general observations concerning the effects of a family split upon children of differing ages. Some authorities feel that divorce has least impact upon children ranging in age from infancy to 3 years, especially if the child stays with its mother.

Most psychiatrists feel that the years from 3 to 6 are the worst ages for children to experience parental divorce. These years are crucial in child emotional development and a mother and father are more necessary to children in this age group than at any other time in their lives. It may be even worse for children whose divorced parents have not explained a father's absence.

Children of divorce who fall into the 6 to 12 age group are usually not nearly as traumatized by parental separation. These children are better able to tolerate change.

Adolescents are even more understanding of a shift in family structure. In general, young people in the 12 to 18-year-old category may not suffer as badly as the younger child would under the same circumstances.

It would seem that the older the child the easier it is to withstand divorce and its consequences to the family. However, studies tend to show that divorce as a whole is a highly individual matter and children's reactions will vary depending upon a multitude of factors: the age of the child, emotional climate in the home, ethnic, religious and cultural background, and what follows after the parents are divorced.

Some children may repress their bad feelings and lie about a divorce in the family. They may pretend the family is still intact. Young children may close their eyes to what they have been told and refuse to believe it. Others may try to ignore it. All of such troubled children may be hoping the family divorce will disappear if they do not admit it is there.

Children will sometimes regress to earlier forms of behavior and begin again to bed wet, to suck their thumbs or use baby talk. In the face of such a monumental family disruption they turn back to prior stages of development. Divorce may cause tremendous feelings of fright as an unknown future looms ahead, and almost any combination of symptoms may appear.

Most reactions are not immediate cause for alarm. It may be your child's method of expressing himself to an internal family explosion.

Usually children will adjust to the divorce and the new arrangement for living in their families in about a year. They even adjust to having mothers, who were formerly at home, work full time if the quality of care they get from a sitter is continuous and the surrogate is interested in them.

For some children, however, the destructiveness of divorce in the family is more than they can bear. If a child does not seem to adjust well to the divorce, continues adverse reactions and is depressed and upset, he may be emotionally ill and in need of treatment. It's a good idea to seek professional help, so his reactions can be channeled in a less destructive way.

The following group of professional helpers are people trained to work with children's problems. They may or may not have a medical degree.

*Psychiatrist:* He is trained as a doctor and has an M.D. degree. After medical school he has specialized in psychiatry and learned to treat emotional disorders through the use of psychotherapy or "talk therapy" or by administering medication. The psychiatrist must know a great deal about the patient's past and present life, as well as his physical condition. Patients are usually treated in the office or may be hospitalized when necessary.

*Psychoanalyst:* Most are trained as doctors and have an M.D. degree. They treat by a form of psychotherapy called psychoanalysis. It investigates human thinking and emotions and delves into individual behavior. The analyst is concerned with personality structure and function and uses the technique of psychoanalysis for treatment. This is usually the most individual and expensive form of therapy.

*Psychologist:* A highly trained psychologist has a Ph.D. degree, which means a degree as a doctor of philosophy. This person has usually studied four years beyond college in the science of human behavior. Many psychologists are trained to administer special kinds of personality tests. Many work in organizations or institutions or schools. *A clinical psychologist* is trained to do therapy with individuals or groups.

*Social Workers:* A social worker has usually studied two years beyond college level work in a graduate school of social work and holds a Master's degree. Their expertise is in the field of interaction between people. They may do therapy in an agency or in private practice.

Within the framework of social work training, those who have had some work in psychiatric facilities may then be referred to as *psychiatric social workers.* Others may have been trained as social workers and have had more work studying the family. Such people may call themselves *family counselors* or *marriage counselors.* Family counselors and marriage counselors are recognized in some states by these names whereas in others they are recognized only as social workers.

All of the previously mentioned specialists are therapists who work toward constructive changes so that a patient's day-to-day living experiences may improve. Treatment can be on an individual basis or can take place in groups. As with any serious illness, cures do not come about overnight. The length of treatment will of course depend on the severity of the problem.

When you go to see a therapist, a parent may inquire about the problem and the possible time of treatment. Ask about fees. Don't be afraid to ask questions. Often it is possible to obtain treatment free of charge or at a minimal charge if the therapy is subsidized by the community or a not-for-profit group. Private practitioners usually charge for their services.

There are many mental health groups, social service agencies and clinics that offer care. It is a good idea to inquire about therapy from a recognized agency. Your child's school, your doctor, your religious leader or other close sources may be able to refer you to reputable individual therapists or to organizations that can provide your family with helpful counseling. If you are in doubt, ask the therapist about his training and background. Anyone in need of therapy should not have to suffer without this kind of assistance so he or she can enjoy an emotionally full and healthy life.

# PART III
# WHEN YOU MARRY AGAIN

# Part 3 Chapter 1
# Preparing the Child

If remarriage is in your future, try to give your children time to adjust to a new parent-figure. Introduce your child to the idea so that the transition, when it comes, can be made with the greatest ease and happiness for all concerned.

* * * * * *

Dorothy hurried her 10-year-old son Jerry. "Come on, Jerry-Berry," she urged with good humor. "Get through with your game. I've got something to tell you."

Jerry looked up at his mother. Something in her voice had aroused his curiosity. "I'll finish later," he said pushing the box aside. "What you got to tell me?"

Dorothy sat down next to her son. "It's about our friend Allen," she said. "You know how much we both like him and you know he comes over often. Well, he likes us, too — in fact he and I have grown to love each other so much that we've decided to get married." She paused to let the idea take hold. "I wanted to tell you *first* before anyone else."

Jerry looked a little puzzled, then troubled. When he finally answered, his questions tumbled out one after the other. "You're going to get married? You are? When?" Then he hesitated. "Mom, does that mean he's going to live with us? What's going to happen?"

His mother hugged him. "We're going to have some new relatives, that's what's going to happen. We'll all be together. You, me, Allen and Nancy." She mentioned Allen's 11-year-old daughter.

"Nancy! Do we have to have her?" Jerry kicked the leg of the table.

"Of course." Dorothy's voice left no doubts. "I wouldn't dream of giving you up because I was getting married, and I'm sure Allen wants his daughter the same as I want you. She's a lovely child and I hope we'll all be a happy family together."

Jerry knitted his eyebrows. He looked down at the floor and didn't answer. "I love you, Son," his mother continued. "I'll be your mom, same as always, and I'll take care of you just the way I always have," she promised.

"But Mom," he sounded troubled. "What about Dad? It'll seem funny for Dad. He's my father. Allen's not my father."

"Of course he's not." Dorothy was very patient. "Allen likes you very much, but he's a friend. He's not your father. You'll still see your dad whenever you like. Your father and I will always be your parents. We both love you. Allen's not going to take away Dad's place."

Jerry kicked the table leg again. "Yes, he is," he insisted. "He's going to take Dad's place with you."

"Dad and I don't have any place with each other any more," Dorothy answered quietly. "Our relationship to each other is finished. You are the only thing we share together and always will." She kissed her son. "Come on, we can talk while I set the table. Allen and Nancy are coming over for dinner."

"It'll seem funny having four people at the table all the time instead of just you and me," There was a wistful quality to Jerry's voice.

"We'll have plenty of time to get used to the idea," Dorothy concluded. "We're not getting married until next spring."

"Oh!" Jerry sounded suddenly relieved.

We'll all have to get used to the idea of being a foursome, Dorothy thought to herself.

* * * * * *

Almost one in three marriages in the United States is a remarriage. Of the million people who divorced last year, most will eventually get married again. Even people with more education and more money, who seem to hit the jackpot for staying married the longest, divorce and remarry in very large numbers.

Children of the remarriage have to make an adjustment to the new family condition just as they did when their parents split up.

After the divorce most kids stay with their mothers. Today's divorcee, though partnerless, tries to keep herself busy. When the first initial shock subsides, the mother usually goes to work and may become involved with limitless activities that she would not have considered just a few years back. The women's liberation movement has opened her eyes to many avenues and there is a need to buffer the fragile marital and financial state with a host of interests. The mother may take up plumbing, auto repairs, wallpapering and wholesale dating.

The child can help with the plumbing or learn auto repairing but rarely is he wanted around when the parent is going out with a date. The child has to adjust to his mother's new friends in the house and he may feel rejected because it cuts into some of the time he may have spent with his mother in her former social state.

If a mother has a lot of short-lived relationships it's just as well that the child doesn't share them. For those who come around with more frequency and for whom the child develops a fond acceptance, it requires emotional juggling to build up to close feelings, and then have to let go if the relationships change with any degree of regularity.

An understanding mother will be discreet in subjecting her child to her friends. She will certainly avoid having her child see or hear her lovemaking. A delicate balance is necessary to let your child know that you are an individual in need of your own life without having him view the highly personal aspects of your friendships.

If you are truly in love with one person who shares your home and family with you, authorities usually find the situation more acceptable for your children than a rotation of people. Very often a friendly lover makes a good parental substitute for a child and becomes a role-model for an absent father who no longer comes to visit.

When you do decide that you will remarry, don't do it "because of the children." Years ago the idea of remarrying for the sake of one's children was very popular. When the sons and daughters grew up and left home the parent was stuck with a mate he or she no longer cared about. It was a poor idea years ago, and it's still bad.

An old fashioned small town widower with seven children decided it was best if he remarried quickly after his wife's death for the sake of the children. Not knowing how to go about finding a new wife who would care for his brood, he permitted an acquaintance to arrange a marriage with a spinster 15 years his senior. The marriage was ill-fated from the onset. The spinster hadn't the slightest idea of how to mother the seven children nor was there any personal attraction between the husband and wife. He had wanted a housekeeper and she had wanted a home.

In time, each child reached adulthood and left the household until the unhappy father was left alone with his dissatisfied wife. It was an unpleasant marriage which ended only at the death of the spinster-wife.

I'd never recommend such a marriage for the sake of the children," the husband confessed, "and I would most assuredly never do it again, either."

Don't look for a fictional prince charming, but find someone who will share your interests, your bed and your family life. When you find him, don't ask your children for permission to remarry. You are the parent. The child is not your mother or father. His agreement to the marriage is not necessary. Neither should you permit your child to manipulate you in the hope of keeping you from remarrying.

However, don't spring the news on your children without groundwork. Try to introduce your husband or wife-to-be to your children so they can build up to some gradual interaction. If you both have children who will be living together, try to let the children become acquainted too.

Talk honestly to your kids about your remarriage. Tell them how you feel and listen to what they say. Consider their feelings just as you did when you told them you and their other parent were divorcing. Reassure them of your love for them and let them know you will all be sharing a life together.

Sometimes children react angrily to such news. Psychologist, Dr. Lillian Vittenson relates one child's conversation upon being told that the mother was going to remarry. "Even if you get married," he blurted out, "my father will always be my father." The child's internal sense of loyalty to his real father may have seemed threatened. Such a child should be reassured that the marriage will not keep him from his relationship with his natural parent.

Reactions to a remarriage, as with every other major situation, will vary with the age of the child. Children who seem unhappy at a parents oncoming marriage should be told again and again that their own position with the parent is solid. It's best if the new stepparent is patient in his attempts to make friends with the child.

Many remarriages work out well. The new marriage extends the family circle with a whole group of relatives. Very often, excellent relationships develop with multiple grandparents, aunts, uncles, etc.... Those second marriages that end in divorce do put a heavy burden on the children who have to experience a family loss for a second time.

However, a parent and his or her children should not enter a new marriage in fear of failure because the old relationship fell apart. Appreciate what there is to be enjoyed today. No one has any reassurance about the permanence of any relationship. Friends move away or our beloved parents die and leave us. Marriages dissolve. The old fears should not be carried into the new experience.

There's as much chance for a successful marriage the second time around as there is the first. In fact many people feel that youthful intransigence is left behind in many second marriages and that there's an even better chance for success because the partners try harder to make things work out.

# Part 3 Chapter 2

# New Stepparents in the House

**Already having to cope with either the death or divorce of one parent, a child with a new stepparent who comes into his life must now make another adjustment. Who is this person? They may ask themselves, will he (she) take my real parent away from me? Will I still be able to see my real mother (father)? The questions can be puzzling and perplexing.**

\* \* \* \* \* \*

Shelley watched them from the doorway. Look at them kissing. Yccch! What does he see in her? And what are they talking about that's so important? I'll bet he'll forget all about me pretty soon with *her* making up to him all the time. Daddy, Daddy! The 14-year-old girl called out silently to her father. Don't forget me. I'm Shelley, your daughter. I need you.

Just then her father spotted her in the doorway. His face lit up with pride as he walked over to greet her. "Here's my big girl." He planted his usual big smoochy kiss on her cheek.

Christy, her new stepmother, greeted her warmly, too. She didn't attempt to kiss Shelley, but she reached out for her hand. "We were waiting for you to come home from your music lesson. Your father and I were trying to decide which movie we'd all like to see tonight, if it's O.K. with you. What's your suggestion?" She sounded genuinely interested in Shelley's answer.

Friday night at the movies? That sounded neat. Shelley was pleased. She mentioned a film she had been dying to see.

"Great!" Dad said. "That's settled. Girls, how about a bite at Culinary Heaven before the movies?" he addressed his wife and daughter.

Culinary Heaven! The evening was getting better and better, Shelley thought. Then she said aloud, "I think I'll wear my new red blouse."

"That looks wonderful on you, dear. I really like it," Christy agreed.

Shelley looked up. Christy seemed sincere in her approval.

Shelley hesitated. "My mother bought it for me."

"She has very nice taste. It's a lovely blouse." Christy complimented her again.

"Oh, *I* picked it out," Shelley assured her. I'm supposed to go shopping for a new pair of jeans tomorrow, too, but Mom can't make it."

"I don't know if I'm as good a shopper as your mother," Christy suggested, "but I'd love to go with you tomorrow. I don't mean to take your mother's place but I'd really enjoy going with you."

She's not so bad, Shelley said to herself in the bathroom mirror as she combed her long blond hair and adjusted the collar on her red blouse. She stuck out her tongue at her image. "I'm going to have a good time tonight with Daddy and Christy."

* * * * * *

When you marry someone with children, you all marry each other. Both the parents and the children who are brought together to form a new family circle have to get used to each other's sounds, smells and habits. It takes effort, but it can be done just as in a very first marriage. Except this time around you may have his or her children, or both, as part of the adjustment.

A stepparent as a family figure is in a peculiar position. The law does not acknowledge any rights for a stepparent. You have rights as a husband or wife, but there are no legal rights vis-a-vis the children of previous marriages that are brought together with the new marriage.

You have no legal position, but you may have plenty of family responsibility taking charge of the household. This is especailly true for a new stepmother, who has chores galore. If there are two sets of children involved, there are double sets of laundry, more cooking, more shopping, more arranging, etc.

One midwest suburban housewife, divorced for the second time, described her chores during her second marriage. Each had brought three daughters into the new household. "Just as I was doing a load of laundry," the mother described, "another bunch would come tumbling down the shoot and hit me on the head as I leaned over the laundry basket. I couldn't take it anymore." Needless to say, there was more amiss with that marriage than excessive laundry.

There aren't any rules for being a successful stepparent. But there are certain unalterable facts—as, for instance, the fact that you are a second-choice mother or father. You're also a second-choice wife or husband. Stepparents have to deal with these psychologically loaded words like being "second" which is not quite as good as being Number One.

Then they have to bear the fact that they are a *step* mother or father. *Step* anything doesn't arouse pleasant visions, since most of us are raised on fairy tales that project evil and step parents into the same bailiwick. If that isn't bad enough, a few other cliches that come out of the old literature and old movies have the stepfather or mother stealing the child's inheritance either by downright thievery or by mesmerizing someone in the family and stealing affection along with the cash. Since divorce has loaded society down with a lot of stepparents, perhaps the old chestnuts will die a gradual death, but there is still an aura of suspicion around the new spouse of a father or mother until some kind of a positive relationship is developed.

In-laws and stepparents are the family interlopers. They marry into it by law but they have no blood ties to the principals and they are affection stealers.

It doesn't seem to be quite as bad if a family gets a new stepfather. He's usually away working, and when he isn't around, which is most of the time, the family continues to function somewhat as it did prior to his intrusion. Of course, if he brings his children into the household, the whole scene is altered and there is another set of problems that need adjusting.

A new stepmother in the house is the one who will have more contact with the children, since it is she who is in charge of the inner workings of the household. The relationships with the stepmother can't help but be more intense than those with a stepfather. Since she's the one who may be making more decisions, there is greater opportunity for her to be resented by "his" children. She may be a father's new wife but she's never the children's new mother — especially if the real mother is somewhere close by. There always are comparisons. Even if the real mother is dead, there often is a resentment that she has usurped the mother's rightful place in the house.

A stepmother and a stepdaughter may be rivals for the father's attention. The principal of a school related her ire at her stepmother when her father remarried. She was a grown woman at the time. "My father and I were extremely close and my stepmother resented that closeness and kept trying to take my father away from me." Her father was long dead but she still remembered her rivalry with the father's wife.

When children become angry at their real parents they may daydream about being someone else's child. They can pretend that somewhere else in the world they have a truly *good* mother or father who wouldn't treat them in such a dastardly way. It's a common fantasy that helps get rid of anger. But along comes someone who in truth is *not* a child's mother and the child becomes angry at her. It destroys his "anger" fantasy; he can't dream of the "bad" mother not really being his mother because she already fits that category. It's very confusing and cuts off this escape route for his ire. Nor does he have the same reasons for accepting unpleasantness as he would from a real parent.

Is having a stepchild akin to adoption? Not really. The motives and emotional involvement is totally different. The legalities are different as well. As stated previously, the stepparent has no legal position of responsibility toward the child. Your relationship with stepchildren is an extension of your relationship with their father or mother. The adopted child usually is raised from birth. Such is not always the case with stepchildren. They already have had one mother or father—whom they miss sorely—before the stepparent arrives on the scene. The other mother or father usually is somewhere around. The adopted child's parents are gone into an unknown mist. Perhaps the desire to solidify the position of stepchildren and stepparents accounts for the many who legally adopt so that they can get away from the fragility of their "step" position.

All is not gloom with stepparents and stepchildren. If there was a lot of unpleasantness between a husband and wife prior to divorce, the children may relish being privy to a happy marriage which improves the interfamily happiness.

Judith Wallerstein and Dr. Joan B. Kelly, who recently have investigated some of the effects of divorce on children, feel that adolescents troubled by their real parents to a point where they may not be playing with their own peers, can improve if they develop a good relationship with a stepparent of remarriage.

Children's ages change the relationships with a stepparent. Becoming a stepparent to very young children is most often easier than with older children. You are more important to a small child. But the older child isn't at home with parents as much and the lessened contact diminishes the importance of the surrogate parent. Adolescents have to be handled with tact and diplomacy.

A child who has lost a parent through divorce will need time to develop a good relationship with a substitute figure. They may be fearful of another loss if things do not work out.

The name of the game is *trying to get along.* You simply have to try to make it work. And let your efforts be known. Let the stepchild know that you want to be fond of him. Don't pretend you are the real mother or you may hear that old invective hurled at you, "You're not my mother. I've got a mother."

Don't compete with the real mother if she's around. Don't attempt to smother the stepchild with kisses and hugs that you don't feel yet. Don't try to buy their affections with new games and toys, or you may set a pattern for pouring out material things forever.

If your stepchild reminds you of the mother or father whom you dislike intensely, try to remember that this child is not an exact replica of only one parent. He also is the child of the parent whom you have married. Don't take it out on the kid because of his genes.

Try to be realistic. This is not your child and you are not going to get married and fall into a fervor of parental love for someone else's child. But if you really try, you can develop a fondness and a liking for each other.

Tread lightly if you are handling the possessions of another mother or father who is out of the house. They may have a lot of meaning for the child.

A son related his sadness at seeing a stepmother alter a silver fruit caddy that his mother had cherished. He recalled her enjoyment of the piece when she used to polish it. "Imagine," he said, "my stepmother didn't even ask anyone about it. She just had a hole drilled into the middle of it and made a lamp out of it. My mother's favorite piece! A lamp!"

On the positive side, sometimes older children will be very happy about a remarriage. They may even be grateful if the new husband or wife relieves them of worry about lonely parents.

Take it easy and go slowly in forming a good relationship with stepchildren. Try to be friendly, really friendly, and be interested in them. It's a gratifying feeling if the friendship grows so that the family members can enjoy good feelings toward each other.

## Part 3 Chapter 3

## Stepbrothers or Sisters

**Remarriage brings the children of the partners together into one family. Through no choice of their own, sons and daughters suddenly find themselves not quite related to a stepparent's children. Whether they like each other or not, they must find the way to family detente, for their position will remain as long as the parents stay married to each other.**

* * * * * *

The noise was tremendous. Shrieks and crying echoed through the hall as Fern and Alex raced into their boys' room.

Mark was trying, amid sobs, to put the pieces back into his dismantled bridge.

"I kicked it by accident." Wayne, the 9-year-old, was aggressive. He explained before they could even ask about it.

"You're always breaking my things." Mark, aged 8, was despondent. "You big bully," he shouted and he ran to Wayne and began to pummel him as hard as he could.

"Stop it!" Alex commanded both boys. "Stop it this minute! I mean it."

"Honey, Wayne didn't mean it." Fern tried to comfort Mark but he refused to be solaced.

He went crying to his father and hugged him. "You see, Dad. She always takes his side. He breaks my things and then she makes excuses for him." His cries became more intense.

Fern shot Alex an apologetic look.

"See here, boys!" Alex was emphatic. "Wayne, you apologize to Mark right now."

Wayne looked to his mother for an answer but she shook her head. "Alex is right, Wayne. Please apologize right now."

"Aw, Mom." Wayne was disgusted. "He's such a little crybaby." He slipped his hands into his pockets.

"Wayne!" His mother was adamant.

"O.K.," he said. "Mark, I apologize." And he stuck his hand out at his stepbrother.

"Go ahead," Mark's father encouraged him. "Take his hand and accept the apology. Now sit down. Both of you!" he commanded. He cleared a spot on Mark's bed and sat down. Fern was next to him and they looked across at the two boys sitting on the other bed.

Alex cleared his throat. "Listen to me, boys," he said. He pointed to Wayne. "I'm not your father." He pointed to his son. "And Fern's not your mother." "But Fern is my wife now and I am her husband. That's not going to change. You boys are not related by blood, but you are stepbrothers for the rest of your lives." Mark started to mumble but Alex stopped him with a restraining glance.

Fern continued the conversation. "We're a family now and we have to learn how to get along, just like you do with the kids in your class at school. You have to be polite to each other and make an effort to be pleasant. We know you have different interests and just as soon as we can afford to move, we're going to try to get a larger apartment where you can each have your own room."

Mark's eyes opened wide and Wayne smiled. "Honest, Mom?" Wayne asked.

Alex answered for her. "Yes, but it will take a little while until we find something that's right for us. In the meantime you have to get along. You must keep trying. We each love you."

"You're very important to us," Fern agreed. "Wayne, you're special to me — and Mark, you're special to your father. You boys always will be. We each love our sons and we're very fond of our stepsons." Both boys looked pleased.

"Now, how about a little dinner?" Fern asked. "I've made everybody's favorite tonight. Fried Chicken and apple pie for dessert."

Each parent gathered up the other's son and they all walked toward the kitchen. "Peace in the house, once more," Alex said. "Let's really try to make it last."

\* \* \* \* \* \*

Each family raises its children in a unique fashion. Every set of parents has its own style of parenting, but with remarriage, lifestyles and tastes are combined and it usually takes concentrated effort to mesh the different parts of the new family into a whole unit. It's especially difficult for kids who not only have to adjust to a new stepparent, but will have to accept new siblings into the bargain.

Redefining the roles in a combined family often is a must.

For instance, if there was only one son in the previous family and now there are two, the positions are altered. It is an adjustment for everyone.

Sometimes one or more of the children may be mourning the loss of the parent from the previous marriage. The new parent must be understanding and encourage the other children in the household to do the same for the grieving members so they eventually can redirect their feelings toward someone else.

One of the biggest problems of a merged family is the competition between the children as they jockey for position in the household. There may be resentments about sharing their space, sharing their lives and sharing their parents. A child who feels very close to one parent and is upset by the loss of the other parent through divorce may become unduly worried about having to share the attention of the remaining parent with intruders into the household.

There is competitiveness between *his* children and *hers*. No matter how they feel, they have to try to make things work out.

It's especially difficult if one child feels that the other is receiving preferential treatment from one of the parents. Very often a stepchild will feel that a real parent sides with his own child, to the detriment of the other.

A young man from Nebraska grew to dislike his stepbrother, who was always shielded from attack by a doting mother. "I was always very fond of my stepsister," he recalled, "but I couldn't stand the way Margaret, my stepmother, always came to Neil's defense. She never admitted he was ever wrong about anything. Actually, she wasn't a bad stepparent, but I just couldn't forgive her for always standing up for Neil against me."

Reverse prejudice also is a problem. Sometimes the real parent will be less harsh with the stepchildren than he will be with his own. If he yells at his own kids but lets the others off with a softer reprimand, not only do his own children resent such uneven treatment, but the other ones may feel uneasy as well.

A family may start out after remarriage with *her* children and a new daddy, never dreaming they will have to cope with *his* children under the same roof. But that is exactly what happens if his children suddenly decide that they want to be part of the household, too. Two sets of children require adjustment after adjustment to make things work.

Even when the arrangement calls for the kids of only one parent to make their permanent home with the newly married couple, the weekends may bring the other set under one roof, too. Sometimes neither parent has the children on a permanent basis but everyone may descend together during the same visiting periods.

Additional children will not only intrude on the privacy of the parents, but they intrude on each other's privacy, not because they are necessarily unpleasant but because there are more people around to get in each other's way. The ecology of the household becomes complicated by this overpopulation with stepchildren.

One mother, who was very conscious of the children's constant intrusion into their personal lives, solved the problem by redesigning the dinner hour. She fed all the children before the husband came home. When the husband arrived, they had a family hour together while the father had a drink and some snacks. After that, the children were encouraged to get on with their own activities while she and her husband dined together. "Dinners used to be a madhouse around here with all the kids together," she recalled. "I didn't want to deprive any of them of my husband, but I felt we needed a little time without any of them. This works out wonderfully, even though I sometimes have to leave the rest of the dishes until morning. It's worth it," she said.

Many strange situations may develop out of a melee of stepchildren. In the division of an estate, for example. Usually, stepchildren do not inherit anything from a stepparent, but often great attachments do occur between parents and a stepchild. One stepmother divided her estate between her own sons and her stepson. "He's just like my own," she explained. "He lived with us from the time he was a sophomore in high school. I wouldn't dream of excluding him in my will."

Sometimes marriages result between stepchildren who have spent time together in one home. "I thought it was the most romantic thing in the world when Bill's son Kevin and my Kathy were married," a Kansas mother explained with joy.

Sometimes a remarriage may bring together children of differing financial backgrounds. If one side of a family, perhaps the grandparents of a divorced parent, is able to provide a great deal of money to a child who is living with stepbrothers or sisters who do not have as much, problems may result in the competition such a situation can promote.

Stepchildren of the same age will occasionally bolster each other's attitudes in a negative way by serving as a model for each other. For instance, if one doesn't want to learn how to swim, the other may decide not to learn either because *Tom doesn't do it*. These children should be encouraged to look to an older person as a pattern for their behavior.

It takes a lot of effort to make stepchildren accept each other, but usually, if the parents are aware of the problems and foster a good attitude in the house, it is easier for the stepbrothers and sisters to adjust to each other. Good relations between stepchildren can extend the family in important and pleasant ways.

## Part 3   Chapter 4

## Worries About Being Disloyal to the Real Mother or Father When You Have a Stepparent

**When one parent remarries, the children may be concerned that their new relationship with the stepparent may interfere with their feeling of loyalty to the old parent. They often are uncomfortable if they worry about the mother's (father's) new spouse stepping into the place of the real parent.**

* * * * * *

Iris looked worried. "If Uncle Spencer comes to my graduation with you, does that mean that Daddy won't be able to come, too?"

Margo ached for her daughter's intense distress. She knew the child worried about her relationship with her own father since her mother and Spencer had married. Spencer wanted so much to be a good stepfather. He hoped that Iris would be a daughter to him, but the more he worked at getting along with Iris, the more she seemed concerned that he was trying to step into her own father's place.

"No thanks, Uncle Spencer," she had told him the other day when he had invited her to attend the King Tut exhibit at the natural history museum.

He had made the offer knowing this was a special interest of his stepdaughter. "I have a membership card so we won't have to stand in line to get in. The three of us will have a great afternoon," he beamed at her, expecting her to be pleased. Instead, somber faced, she had rejected the suggestion at once.

"My father and I are going to go together," Then she added, "He said he'd take me and I want to go with my father."

Spencer hadn't said anything at first, but he had been hurt by her blunt refusal. Later that night he had complained to his wife. "No matter what I suggest, it seems she's always worried that it will show some kind of disloyalty to her father if she accepts my idea. I don't want to be her father. But I do want her to like me and I'd like to be a special kind of friend."

Margo, confronted now by her daughter, was concerned about Spencer's reaction to Iris's graduation. He had planned to go and had even talked of a gold neck chain he had seen at a jeweler's as a possible graduation gift.

"I thought I'd talk it over with you first before we got it for her," he had said. He was so anxious to please.

Margo mulled over a possible solution. "Maybe you can ask for an extra ticket to the graduation," she suggested finally to her daughter.

Iris frowned. "Why does Uncle Spencer always have to come too? He's not my father. I've got a father. I don't need another one," she concluded.

"Iris!" Margo was stunned. "He's my husband. You live with us, and he tries so hard to be your friend. Why do you always try to shove him aside?" Then she stopped herself from going on any further. She realized that the child was confused and anxious about not losing her own father.

"Iris," Margo tried to explain. "Your own father loves you very much. Spencer will never take his place and he doesn't want to. He just wants to have a really good relationship with you and be a special kind of friend. He's not trying to push your father out of his rightful place."

"Does he have to go to the graduation if I can't get another ticket?" Iris wanted to know.

Margo sighed, "Of course not. Uncle Spencer's not going to take away your father's ticket. He thought there would be one for him, too, but if there isn't, I hope he'll understand." Iris seemed much happier as she switched on the T.V.

She would have to talk to Spencer, Margo thought, and ask him to cool it with Iris. Spencer would have to win Iris's confidence and friendship, but he'd have to do it in such a way that Iris didn't think he was elbowing her real father out of the picture.

"Iris, I want to try to make you understand that there is room for family friends in our affections, too." Margo started to explain. "Let me repeat, Spencer does does not want to replace your own father. He just wants to develop his own good relationship with you. He doesn't want to stop you from ever being with your dad." Margo knew that she would just have to tell her daughter over and over again until Iris did understand. And of course, she hoped Spencer would understand as well.

* * * * * *

Children usually are anxious to be loyal to their parents and to love them. In return they want parents to love them and to feel good about their children. When one of the parents remarries and the child's family begins to consist of three or more parents, there may be a problem to the child about remaining loyal to the original cast of parents. Having two kinds of parents of the same sex, a real father and a stepfather, can cause concern to a child who feels they are competing for his attention and affections. If the child develops a good relationship with a mother's husband, he may worry that this may make him disloyal to his own father.

Loyalty conflicts vary with the age of children and the particular situation in the house. Younger children, such as those from ages 5 to 10, are dependent upon their parents for emotional support and feel very much attached to them even after divorce. They may suffer very keenly from any situation that makes them feel disloyal in any way to their real parent.

Older children who imagine themselves to be disloyal to an original parent in reality or in fantasy may feel squeezed by the emotional impact. They then could be resentful of *all* the parents for putting them into such an untenable position. Adolescents sometimes adapt to uncomfortable situations with stepparents or parents by avoiding discussions of each with the other or even lying when it serves their own needs for self esteem.

Ultimately the older child may try to back away from conflicts of loyalty by not getting involved.

It's not a good idea for a stepparent consciously to compete with a real parent no matter how much he wants to get along with the child. It's wonderful for child and stepparent to develop a working rapport but if the child resents the new parent's efforts, the stepparent has to rethink his position. Very often these are matters of degree of feeling and require tact and understanding. Ambivalence that the child feels should be worked out so that a comfortable relationship with all the principals can result.

Never should any child be encouraged to favor one real parent or even a stepparent over the other real parent. Forcing such a decision on a child only serves to make him feel angry, guilty and depressed.

Feeling disloyal toward a parent creates *guilt*, an unhealthy condition that causes a child many unnecessary problems. Wherever possible, parents should help children overcome such reactions. Children are less able than adults to handle new relationships. Therefore, it is often more difficult for them to resolve alone the complex problems of new family interminglings.

At times, even adults cannot overcome a sense of divided loyalties. A California attorney recalled how he felt when his father remarried long after the mother's death. The father had struggled for financial success during the early years of his first marriage. When he remarried at middle age, he had achieved his goal of owning several appliance stores and was well able to afford many luxuries for the new wife he had not been able to afford for the first one. Soon after the father's remarriage, the stepmother's birthday rolled around and the father asked his son's advice in selecting a diamond watch for the new spouse.

"Which one should I buy for Elsa?" the father asked, showing three elaborate watches to the son. The son recalled his own mother's thin, worn, gold plated watch. "Pick it out yourself," he told his father in a rather testy manner.

"How could I make that choice for him?" he told his wife later. "It seemed so disloyal to help my father select that kind of a gift for Elsa when he'd never given my own mother anything that fine!"

Children are committed to their own parents. Whenever there is any kind of a confrontation between a real parent and a stepparent, the child is almost always going to side with his original parent.

A great deal of the attitudes that children will have toward stepparents and their ability to handle guilt and loyalty feelings will emanate from the attitude of their real parents. If the mother who has remarried has a constructive feeling toward the child's relationship with her ex-spouse and the ex-husband is positive in his attitudes toward the new husband, it is much easier for the child to accept them all.

If the father says, "Glad you got to see the circus with

your mother and her husband. Come on, help me wash my car," the child will know that the father is not angry or competing for his company at the circus. But if the same father says, "Oh, so you went to the circus with your mother and her husband. How come? You knew *we* were going to go," or "You had a good time at the circus with *them?*" " That father is putting doubt in his child's mind about having gone to the circus without this parent. The father's comments are guilt-producing and would make a child feel he had been disloyal to his real father.

Of course, parents cannot forfeit their own lives completely for their children, nor should they pander to a child's feelings of selfishness with excessive gratification, but unless there is a special circumstance to the contrary, the child's needs usually should be considered before the needs of the parents. The parents are adult. Having lived longer, they should be more adept in balancing the problems of life. Children need to be guided and taught by them so they too can develop and mature in their life experiences.

When a parent remarries, there is some feeling that children should not be present at the remarriage, the thinking being that if the child enjoys himself at the wedding and then remembers the parent who was not there, it may cause him to feel he has been disloyal. Others, to the contrary, feel that the child should share in something this important to the family and that he should not be left out. Whatever a family decides about a remarriage should depend on the attitude of the individual child and what would seem to make him most comfortable.

A new stepparent should understand that he or she and the real parent who was formerly in his or her position cannot help but be rivals, but that this is not an insurmountable position. He or she can lessen the rivalry by not treading on the territory of the original parent vis-a-vis the child. The new stepparent shouldn't pretend that the old parent doesn't exist. Neither should he put himself in a position of telling the child what to do when that child has already been instructed by the original parent. Such a situation can only cause children to feel divided loyalties. The real parent who has remarried should never force the child to be extremely loving to a new stepparent nor insist that the child call the stepparent "Mom" or "Dad." If there is a real mom or dad around, the child will almost certainly feel this as a mark of disloyalty to his own parent.

Good feelings for a stepparent should develop gradually. They cannot be forced. The new stepmother or stepfather should be himself and should try to encourage friendship without trying too hard to be the "good guy," but he should let the child know at the same time that the friendship is never intended as a replacement for the real parent.

The efforts should be continuous and should be repeated over and over until the child comes to understand that a good relationship with a stepparent does not make him disloyal to his own parent.

## Part 3  Chapter 5

## Worries About Seeing the Real Parent if the Other Parent Remarries

Children often worry about their continuing relationship with parents after divorce. If the mother or father they live with remarries, they may be even more concerned about maintaining their contacts with the out-of-house parent, especially if it seems to them that the new marriage will alter their status with that parent.

* * * * * *

As Martin hung his coat and hat in the front closet, his eyes scanned the mail on top of the hall table. He could tell by the way it was ruffled about that Madeline, his 10-year-old daughter, had been looking through it again.

Damn that woman! He thought about Diana, his first wife. Why couldn't she write to their daughter? Didn't she understand that the girl felt abandoned not hearing from her for so long? Diana never understood anyone, least of all Madeline, he thought to himself.

She had left their daughter in Martin's custody after the divorce, explaining that she was going to be too busy with her photography assignments in Europe to raise her. "You're better at parenting than I am," she had pronounced, and Martin had to agree. But she had kept in contact with Madeline quite regularly—for Diana. About once a month. However, since Martin and Muriel had married three months ago, Diana seemed to have dropped out of the picture as though his marriage were the cause. Martin was certain this was not the case, but Madeline was becoming increasingly worried. She scrutinized the mail delivery every day.

Often when he came home, Martin found his daughter in her room hunched over her desk writing on her white and blue birthday stationary. Only yesterday Madeline had asked her father if Zurich was spelled with a k. Zurich had been Diana's last known address.

Today, as usual, he found his daughter upstairs, her long, dark hair spread across the desk like a fan as she leaned over the letter she was writing.

"Hi Posie," Martin said using his pet name for Madeline.

"Daddy!" Madeline rose from her chair and wrapped herself around her father's waist. She hugged him with all her might and seemed reluctant to disengage herself.

"Who are you writing to?" he asked, trying to sound casual.

"Oh, no one." Then she hesitated. "I thought I'd write to Mommy."

Martin seized the opportunity to talk about Diana. Madeline, he thought, had mourned her mother long enough. "I don't know why you don't hear from your mother, but I know one thing. It's not because you aren't a wonderful and loving daughter. I don't know what your mom is caught up with right now that's keeping her from writing, but she'd probably write if she could." He kissed the top of his daughter's shiny hair. "I just want you to know there are lots of people who love you besides your mom; there's your grandmother, your grandfather, your Aunts Glynis and Marilyn." He counted them off on his fingers. "And of course, there's always and forever, *ME!*"

Madeline smiled in an uneasy way. Finally, she blurted out, "But Dad, maybe Mom thinks I don't need her anymore because Muriel is here." The girl looked down at her shoes, embarrassed at her disclosure.

Martin shook his head. "Your mother didn't forget to write because I got married. I'm positive it hasn't anything to do with that," he assured her. "That's just the way she is." Then he shrugged. "Let's go down to dinner." Arm in arm Martin and his daughter descended the stairs.

It was like a vindication, Martin thought, when a letter from Diana arrived for Madeline the next day.

"Please tell your father too," she had written. "I know what a worry wart he is. I just got hung up with some work. There's nothing wrong if I don't write. And congratulate him on his marriage, for me."

\* \* \* \* \* \*

The worries that a child may have about seeing an out-of-house parent after the remarriage of the other parent often

# DADDY DOESN'T LIVE HERE ANYMORE

are complicated by existing anxieties. A child also can be troubled that a remarriage by either parent will bring other children or stepchildren to replace him in the parent's affections and destroy his relationships. Or he may worry that the absent parent disapproves of the new stepparent and that this will alter their visits together.

Remarriage activates a sense of rivalry with stepparents especially between stepparents and children of the same sex. It may create a fear that this new diversion will subvert the real parent from being attentive to the child. Since the child who lives with one parent already is in physical proximity to him, it is obvious that he will have more contact anxieties about the parent he does not see all the time.

Boys and girls want to feel they are part of their mothers and fathers even when they aren't together all of the time. They always want to know they have parental love and support. The may worry when any circumstance interferes wich their needs.

Older children's desire to be protected by the parents is in opposition to the independent mobility they seek as they are growing up. Nonetheless they need the safety and security of a life line to the mother and father as they strike out on their own. They sense the loss of such an anchor when one parent is absent.

Whether or not a remarriage is involved, many a child's fears about not seeing one of the parents are justified. Surprising numbers of parents stop seeing their children after divorce even though they may or may not continue to lend them financial support. Low-income parents frequently are out of touch with their natural children following a dissolution of a marriage, but even higher-income families may react as through the children, too, were divorced.

Melinda, a strikingly beautiful woman from New Mexico, was divorced by her college professor husband. The following year she remarried. Tom, her ex-husband, has since seen their four children only once a year. When questioned, the father was self-righteous about having minimized his visits with his children. Despite the fact that he was an educated man, he seemed unconcerned about the emotional and financial needs of his growing sons and daughters. He counted himself as a middling kind of parent even though he so seldom saw his children. He could not understand why his ex-wife felt he had divorced his children as well as their mother.

Not all loss of contact with a parent is undesirable. In chaotic situations it frequently is helpful to sever relations with an unmanageable parent.

One teenager, relating her reactions to her mother's divorce from an alcoholic father, described it as sheer relief. Her mother, a handsome midwest executive of a large firm, said her only regret was that although she personally was now rid of her ex-husband, she hoped that the burden of dealing with the father's emotional problems would not later come to rest at her daughter's door. "It's so wonderfully peaceful now," she explained, "and my daughter can grow up in a much more pleasant atmosphere. But as she gets older I hope she won't have to answer all those unpleasant calls relating to my ex-husbands' behavior. The last time we were notified before the divorce, he was on a plane dead drunk and the airline didn't know what to do with him in that condition. It required all manner of complicated arrangements to get him back home. I hope my daughter won't some day have to take up where I've left off. She's out of touch with him now, and I hope she stays that way."

A child's worry about not seeing the other parent after a remarriage may relate to the mourning he feels about the break up of the original marriage. The new marriage can exacerbate this feeling of sadness.

Tied up with children's worries about not seeing their parents are all the seemingly real bogey men of guilt and fear of abandonment that follow divorce. It can be worse for younger children who may develop a serious depression if they are unable to handle their sense of loss.

Guilt is crushing for a child who worries that his bad thoughts toward a parent caused the absence. Anger and rage will often make a child wish his parents would die and disappear. If the parent subsequently leaves, the child may feel his wishes were to blame and he is anguished by guilt.

Children often equate a parental absence with a lack of love for them. If a child feels unloved, he may be unable to love anyone else in return. Later in life it can affect an adult's ability to develop a successful relationship with a mate of the opposite sex. A daughter whose father leaves her early in life, may feel an unconscious worry that others will reject her, too. Her reactions may be,"I don't want a man. They aren't nice to me." Or she may go in the other direction and seek a father in every man she meets. A son whose mother has left him at an early point in his life sometimes runs into similar problems with other women at a later time.

There are other varied reactions that can occur in divorce and remarriage. In one case a son left an overly devoted mother to live with a remarried father.

The highly neurotic mother had always been dependent upon him. With the breakup of the marriage, her attentions to the son became stifling. She would beg him not to leave her as his father had done. She reminded him always that he was her only son. Every utterance only served to make the son more guilty and unhappy.

The boy revolted when he entered high school and went to live with the father. His departure caused such bad feelings with the mother that he did not see her again until the day of his wedding.

When the mother arrived at the nuptials, she belabored the loss of contact with her son. "This is the first time I've seen my only son in years," she told everyone.

"If I had known she was going to carry on again like she used to, I never would have asked her to come," the son complained.

Most often, however, loss of contact with a desired parent is painful and interferes with a child's basic trust and faith in people.

A mother should encourage a child with such fears to be rational and accept a "wait and see" attitude before making assumptions about the absence of the other parent.

If the parent truly doesn't come around anymore and intends to remain out of contact with the child, whether or not it relates to the mother or father's remarriage, the at-home parent should consider the welfare of the child before her own anger or irritation. If she can contact the ex-husband to discuss the handling of the child's fears she should do so. If this is not possible, the remaining parent, as always, has to handle the situation in the most reasonable fashion.

A good relationship with a stepparent can soften the blow that is sensed by a child who feels abandoned by one parent. A stepfather or stepmother often is a successful surrogate for the absent parent and can serve as a role-model in the child's development.

The most pressing need is to make the child know that he is loved. Authorities differ on whether you should or should not say that the absent parent really does love the child if it is questionable. Psychiatrist Dr. Richard Gardiner feels it is pointless to tell a child that a parent who hasn't come to see him in five years really loves him. Other psychiatrists feel it may help a child to feel lovable and loved. He has to know that whether or not there was a remarriage, and whether or not he does see both parents all the time, he is a person who is worthy of love from someone and that there are people who love him all the time and always will.

## Part 3   Chapter 6

## What Do You Call the New Stepparent?

A stepparent joins a family that is already formed, and his relationship to stepchildren emanates from the parent whom he has married. Sometimes the title or designation for this new person that children will use in referring to him is spontaneous. Other times it may require a thoughtful decision.

* * * * * *

"Mom, it was awful," Hope told her mother.

Martha looked at her with surprise. "I thought you wanted Phil to go to the Girl Scout party with you? What's wrong? What happened?"

"Nothing happened," her daughter asserted. "The party was great!"

"Well then, what was the matter?" Her mother was concerned. "Was it Phil? Did he do something?"

"Gee, no Mom," Hope seemed to be struggling to explain. "It was that game we played. I didn't know what to call him."

Martha furrowed her eyebrows. "What game? I don't understand what you're saying."

"It was an introducing game. Every time the piano stopped playing we had to change seats and introduce our parents to the new people we sat next to. And I never knew what I should call Phil."

Her mother laughed with relief. "Oh, is that all."

"It's not funny." Hope was indignant.

"I'm not laughing at you." Her mother assured her. "I just thought it was something much worse."

"But Mom, sometimes when I introduced him I called him my mother's friend, Phil. Once I called him Mr. Glenner and another time I said he's going to be my stepfather soon. I just didn't know how to say it. Phil said not to worry and just call him anything at all but I felt stupid. What *should* I call him, Mom?"

Martha thought for a minute. "Well, you could say my mother's husband-to-be, or my soon-to-be stepfather or my

161

Uncle Phil or just Phil. Why don't you just refer to him as my stepdad?"

Hope folded her Girl Scout kerchief. "I don't want to call Phil *step* anything. I like him and that sounds like he's bad or something."

Her mother smiled. "I don't agree with you. I think that's old fashioned. There are lots of nice stepparents nowadays, but it's O.K. with me. What do you *want* to call him?"

"Just Phil, I guess. That's what I've always called him but I thought now that you're going to get married that it wouldn't be right anymore for an 11-year-old girl to call her mother's husband by his first name."

"It's perfectly all right," her mother assured her. "As long as Phil doesn't mind and it makes you comfortable, Phil is what you'll go on calling him. If you need to explain more than that, just say this is Phil, my mother's husband. How's that?" she concluded.

"Oh that's much better, Mom. I hope I won't get all mixed up about it again." She kissed her mother and added, "I forgot to tell you, *Phil* said he'll call you in an hour."

* * * * * *

New stepparents can be described as acquired parents, new parents, chosen parents, parents-by-marriage, my father's wife, my mother's husband, Marion's husband or Harold's wife ad infinitum. The choice of description depends on the child's preference. Problems arise because a mother and father are most commonly called Mom, Dad, Mother, Father, etc. . . Each language has an equivalent name by which children may refer to their parents, but there isn't a satisfactory appelation for stepparents.

Variations are endless and depend on the preference of the individual and the circumstances of family choice. One is not more correct than the other. It's personal.

Often children do not wish to refer to a stepparent as their mother or father if the real parent is alive and also part of their lives. They may vary it by saying, Dad Henry for the stepfather or Mother Ruth for the father's wife.

Grandparent names sometimes require similar choices. If there are more than one set of grandparents, one grandmother may be Grandma Evelyn and the other may be Grandma Fannie. There are all kinds of combinations of loving names

# DADDY DOESN'T LIVE HERE ANYMORE

for the parents of parents.

One grandson called his grandfather by a first name, Sam. Whereas the grandmother was Grandma. The granddaughter in that very same family call her grandfather, Pa and referred to the grandmother as Gram. Each person finds his own way to indicate family members. It's a good idea to let it work out the same way with stepparents.

Last name choices can become more complex at times if families dislike having their children known by differing surnames. This is often cited as one of the common reasons for legal adoption of stepchildren.

Some parents feel a single name serves to indicate a unified family. If the children are minors this can only be arranged with the approval of the natural living parent.

There have been many times when stepchildren have insisted on name changes in the courts without adoption. One doctor's stepdaughter went to court on her eighteenth birthday and changed her last name as a mark of love and respect for the stepfather.

There have been name changes to defy a real parent who hasn't been attentive to a child. The child will change his last name as a public avowal of disassociation with the real mother or father. Name changes in the courts should be well thought out to make sure that it is truly the choice of the individual and not a whim of the moment.

Some stepparents feel it is a mark of the highest acceptance for a child to refer to them as "Mom" or "Dad". But it's not a good idea to force a child to refer to stepparents as a mother or father, especially if the child has his own natural parent and resents having to call a stepparent by such a personal term. He may feel the name competes with a biological parent. Let the term be the child's spontaneous choice.

There is ambivalence about the use of the word *step* because ot dredges up a bad image. The stepparent is burdened with a loaded word from the onset of his relationship. Most people are raised with fairy tales that bring an ugly picture of an unpleasant person to mind.

But occasionally even a variation of *Mother* or *Father* may be a mark of confusion. One boy, whose divorced father had a constant succession of mistresses, did not know how to refer to the stream of new women who inhabited his father's house. Finally he began to call them *Mommy*, each in turn, although his own mother remained, "Mom"

Divorce has not only caused name problems for children. It has often made it difficult for the people with whom divorced people deal. One busy obstetrician-gynecologist observed that sometimes cross-references are required in his office because divorce is so prevalent in his practice. The same patient may have the birth of three children noted on her records, each fathered by someone with a different last name. "In some cases," he commented, "there are so many erasures of names and addresses that it requires a great deal of extra work to keep the patient records current."

Tell a child that it is not important what he calls a stepparent. "Tell the child to refer to stepparents in any way that makes him comfortable," says Dr. Seymour Pastron. "Let the child use the stepparent's first name if he wants suggests Ruth Rubinstein, marriage and family counselor. It is much more important for children to feel good about that person than to refer to them with endearments that they do not feel. Explain that the stepparent is not a real parent and is not there to replace the real parent. Let children know that the stepparent is an additional member of a family and that, hopefully, all will be able to develop pleasant feelings regardless of how each addresses the other.

Suggest names to your child if he seems confused about what to call a stepparent but let him make his own choice if he does not like the one you've made for him. Assure him that he can change the stepparent's name later on if he decides to make it "Uncle John" instead of just "John", or he can go by the stepparent's last name without a legal change if that works out best. The spirit of the name is far more important than the name itself.

## Part 3 Chapter 7

## Concern About Money for Your Child When You Remarry

The financial problems relating to your child go on even when you remarry. Will the real father continue to support his child? Will the new stepfather mind if he has to spend additional money for the extra person in the house — your child? The answers are indeed cause for concern for all the parents involved.

\* \* \* \* \* \*

Geraldine sat at the desk, resting her head in her hands. She read Albert's note over again. Why had she been so stupid? Why hadn't she figured out the child support angle a little better before she and Bob had eloped? They had been so happy at finding each other that she had been too entranced to think about the practical part of their union; such as who was going to support Vicki, her 9-year-old daughter. How could she have been so impulsive? Albert had been overjoyed at her remarriage. He had sent her a very nice note of congratulations and had enclosed her check—a substantially reduced amount. She stared at it in disbelief. Most of her money from Albert, her ex, had been given to her as alimony, not as child support. Just thinking about it gave her a headache.

Vicki came bouncing in from school, her eyes shining with happiness. "Mom," she was rapturous. "You know the practice flute lesson I've been taking at school? Well, the teacher said I was so *good* for a beginner! They want me in the orchestra. I can rent the flute for now, and later I can buy one. Mom, it's *so* neat. I never thought I'd like it but it's *so* neat," she repeated.

Flute lessons! Geraldine tried to calculate the cost, but aloud she said, "That's nice." She looked at her daughter's enthusiastic glow. She's been so happy since she started. How can I deny her such happiness? How much did a flute cost, she wondered? And lessons? How much were they?

"Be sure to call your father, and tell him all about your

new interest," she encouraged her daughter. "Ask him if it's O.K."

For a moment Vicki's face clouded. "Mom, what if he says I can't do it? He'll let me, won't he?" She reassured herself and kissed her mother and headed for some milk and cookies in the kitchen.

Geraldine felt a lump in her throat. She wanted to cry. She knew Albert, and she wasn't at all sure he would increase the allowance for Vicki without a court fight. But she couldn't lay this on Bob. It wouldn't be fair. She loved him too much. He was already burdened with payments to *his* ex-wife for *their* three children. How could she ask him to spend extra money on Vicki? Yet, how could she deny her daughter?

She thought of all the things she should have decided before, such as who would pay for Vicki when they all went out together? Who would pay for the extra groceries it took to keep Vicki in milk and cookies? Who would pay for the visits to the doctor? She had always been almost certain that Albert would pay for the super big necessities, such as braces on Vicki's teeth. It was all the little things that bugged her. Like the extra pairs of gym shoes and the extra school money and now the flute lessons. She could just hear Albert's voice coming back to her. "Well, you'll just have to make do, won't you, Toots?" She hated it when he called her "Toots".

Well, she had two alternatives. She had always worked on a part-time basis, but maybe now she would work full time to make up the extra money she'd need. The other possibility was to demand that Albert pay more support for their child.

Why not? she thought to herself. Why should Albert get off the hook that easily? The thought infuriated her. She'd talk to him first, and if that didn't work, she'd see Mr. Bressler, her lawyer. But that would take money, too. Anyway, she would try to reason with Albert before she did anything else. She knew one thing for sure, she wasn't going to jeopardize her relationship with Bob. She would try very hard to keep his expenditures for Vicki at a minimum.

She sighed and reached for the phone. "Is Mr. Albert Miller there?" she inquired. She sat up straight and girded herself for the fight.

* * * * * *

Second marriages create complex bookkeeping for a new

family. There is *our* money, *his* money if he's supporting a former wife and their kids together and *her* money if she's receiving child support from children of a previous marriage. If the new wife works to help out, there is *her* income added to *his*. But if she syphons off part of it for *her* children, that requires another pigeon hole. The suit for the new family must have a lot of different pockets.

If you figure out the finances of a new living arrangement in advance, you can ease these problems of the remarraige. Stepparents have no legal obligation to support stepchildren. Yet it becomes almost impossible to calculate that you need an extra quarter of a pound of bologna for your son's lunch or that his daughter eats more raisins than anyone else in the house. And how about the extra costs of going camping with the stepkids or skiing or entrance fees for a family day at a museum? Can you document every extra ice cream cone a stepparent buys for the spouse's children? The practical result is that a stepparent almost always winds up paying for some part of the day-to-day living expenses of a new wife's children who live with him.

Even if the kids don't live with you, how about the weekends or vacations they do spend with you? Are you going to be able to get down to the nitty-gritty of what the extra costs are for this part-time family member?

If a stepfather does not object to paying for part of a child's support, it may give him a feeling of having the right to make certain decisions for the child. Such feelings of responsibility will sometimes make the new family seem more unified. If the real father pays all of the expenses for a child, the stepfather often feels "out of it," and like a perpetual third party.

Most second wives have to work, especially when there are support payments to be met for former families. The working in itself doesn't seem to create additional problems. First-time married, working wives who are mothers don't seem to be any more dissatisfied or have any more problems than married mothers who go to work the second marital time around. As a general rule, wives are more financially dependent on husbands than the reverse. A woman who needs additional funds for *her* children, but is unable to work because the children are too young, must look to one of her husbands for monetary help.

"Mommy says she can pay for only one sleeve so you'd better pay for the rest of the jacket," a young New York son told his real father. "I need a new one. My old one from last year is too small on me."

If you have older children from a previous marriage, they may be able to make the arrangements for their needs alone. It may not be necessary for a parent to intercede on their behalf with an ex-husband or ex-wife. Older children usually are made aware of the difference in financial matters after a divorce and a subsequent remarriage.

An ex-wife can be irritated by the money a former husband spends on his stepchildren. It is just as upsetting for the new wife to stand by and watch her husband's meager paycheck go to cover his outings with his children from a former marriage.

One mother developed her own money-saving scheme for spending time with her own children of divorce when they visited. "We usually have a homework hour. My boys bring their books over. My daughter lives with me all the time because my ex and I have a split custody arrangement. So my daughter and I sit down around our kitchen table with the boys. The kids all do their homework while I figure out the expenses for the week. Usually I bake them something special and then we have a milk and cake party together. But we don't go in for expensive activities. I can't afford it and I don't feel that's the most important part of being together, anyway."

The circumstances of a stepfather raising his wife's child and educating him is known as *in loco parentis*. That indicates that the spouse's son or daughter has been treated as a child in the family. But the condition is still not binding upon the stepparent, who can terminate the relationship at any time. A few states require stepparents to help support stepchildren. New York and California will do so if a child becomes the ward of the state and the stepparent does not support him. Such rulings are always subject to change, depending on the voting in state legislatures.

There is usually small concern that a stepchild will inherit any money in the family. Occasionally they do become the inheritors, depending on personal relationships.

One Texan left the bulk of his estate to his wife's granddaughter, much to the consternation of his brother's children, who had always assumed they would be his heirs. The granddaughter, in turn, left her money to a stepson when she died. She, too, had cousins who had expected to inherit from her.

The best way to avoid the financial blues over your child when you remarry is to have it all spelled out in advance. Have your attorney and your accountant help you determine how to handle the support for your children before you marry someone else. They can look into taxes and any retirement or Social Security benefits that your ex-husband will receive. However, there is usually small direct gain in these matters for an ex-wife; but it may be helpful for the children.

If your new husband-to-be has a lot of money, he may arrange a pre-nuptial agreement. This is a written agreement that will act as a safeguard for the child you may have together if your new marriage doesn't work out. It may also guarantee specified amounts to be paid to you at the termination of your marriage.

A highly publicized pre-nuptial agreement was that made by tycoon Aristotle Onassis with Jacqueline Kennedy and her children by President John F. Kennedy. Upon Onassis' death the new widow and her children received a pre-arranged portion of his gigantic estate.

Almost always the real father is looked to for a child's support. Make out a list of what is needed. Will the father's payments cover all of the expenses? If not, arrange for him to increase payments. If he can't or won't, make certain that the new husband understands what is involved in the matter of caring for your children. Be realistic in your projections. Include baby sitters, if you need them. Don't let support money for your children be a bone of contention in your new marriage. Be reasonable and honest. It will pave the way to a smoother life with a new husband.

## Part 3   Chapter 8

## Discipline From the Stepparent

**Who is going to rebuke a naughty stepchild? How do you control a child's bad behavior if you are a stepparent? The answers are important, though knotty, for the family that is made up of one original parent and one newcomer to this parental scene.**

* * * * * *

Marjorie's head was pushed so far forward it looked as though her ears were standing straight out in defiance. "You're not my mother," she screamed at Joella. "You can't make me."

Joella swallowed and closed her eyes. She wanted to swat the child across the face. She had worked so hard all day getting the house ready for a visit by David's boss, yet here was Marjorie leaving her mess of a puzzle all over the floor right in the very room she planned to use for cocktails before dinner. "Marjorie," Joella's voice was firm. "I know I am not your mother, but I am in charge of the house and you cannot keep your puzzle on the floor tonight. Your father and his boss will be here soon for dinner. It will not be comfortable for anyone if they have to step across your toys to sit down."

Marjorie complained as she backed away from her position. "You don't make Davey take his toys away." Her tone was bitter. "It's because he's your son and I'm not your daughter."

Joella was aghast. This was a new wrinkle in their relationship. Marjorie had never seemed this jealous of Davey before. She crossed over and tried to put her arm around the little girl. "Honey, your brother Davey is only 1½-years-old. When he's 7, he's going to have to pick up his toys, too. Indeed, he will." Then she tried to appeal to her stepdaughter. "I know how close you are to finishing this jigsaw puzzle and I'm truly sorry you have to take it off the floor. Your father and I will try to help you with it tomorrow night, how about it?" she coaxed.

By now Marjorie was crying. She used the back of her

hand to wipe her eyes. "Will you and Daddy really help me tomorrow night?"

Joella nodded as she started toward the pieces with a box. "We'll even set it on the card table in your room so you can keep it up as long as you like."

That seemed to placate Marjorie, who finally began to remove the small pieces off the floor.

Tonight wouldn't be a good time to talk it over with David, but something would have to be done about Marjorie, Joella thought. She just couldn't go on being defiant and willful. Joella felt in her bones that it would be best that discipline be administered by David. He was going to have to let Marjorie know that there were ground rules in the house and that she had to obey them. She hoped that David would agree with her. But for now she had better feed Davey and finish the hors d'oeuvres.

"That looks so much better," she told her little stepdaughter after awhile. "Thank you. Now, come help me squeeze the cream cheese on the crackers while I feed Davey. You make such good squiggles." And she led the little girl into the kitchen.

\* \* \* \* \* \*

All children are naughty and in need of discipline sometimes. Although they need a certain amount of freedom of choice during their development, children also need to learn what is acceptable and what is unacceptable social behavior. It's often extremely difficult for these lessons and the necessary restraints to come from a stepparent.

If a parent and a stepparent cooperate, they should lay down the ground rules for certain attitudes in the house. It is much easier for the child to accept the regulations if both parents are in agreement. The authority that a stepparent has must derive from the real parent. If this parent supports the position of the stepparent in the family definition of acceptable behavior, it makes for a much smoother running home.

One of the difficulties with disciplining a stepchild is that the stepparent must be somewhat more gentle than he would be with his own children. Discipline cannot be handled in quite the same way with a spouse's child. There are many rebukes that one accepts from real parents that are hard to accept from a stepparent. The real parent is in a permanent and never ending position, even in death. The stepparent is in a tenuous position. There is an impermanent quality to the relationship that must be cultivated to develop a firm footing.

Children are dependent on their parents for everything; food, care, clothing and emotional security through love. The withdrawal of love from a naughty child is a punishment. Coming from a stepmother, the threat of this kind of punishment can seem very threatening to a child who may already feel unloved because the real parent has left him. It often is difficult for a child to develop good feelings about a stepmother, or stepfather if he feels that he is being punished unjustly for bad behavior.

Most stepparents are well aware of their fragile position with the child and they are reluctant to play the *heavy* in the family.

Stepmothers of young children have a harder time stepparenting than most stepfathers. Mothers always play a more powerful role in the lives of children. From birth on, they are the ones who feed the child and spend much time with them. When a stepmother has to play the surrogate, much more is expected of her than a stepfather. There are many times when the attention and needs of stepchildren create a very close bond with a stepmother.

The daughters in a suburban family became very much attached to their stepmother. She assumed all of the responsibility for raising them. She praised them, cleaned them, fed them and disciplined them. Later, when the father and stepmother divorced, the children still continued to see their stepmother. "Even when I punished them, those kids knew I loved them. They are almost grown now and they still come over. They even have keys to my house." the stepmother explained.

Stepfathers, knowing their role is often less important, may feel like a third wheel with a wife's children and refuse to involve themselves in family skirmishes. The price of such nonintervention is that the child sometimes comes to view the stepfather as a person who is not interested because he does not care enough about his wife's children.

One mother who was questioned about the conduct of her new husband toward her children said, "He doesn't really matter. The kids don't ever think of him, because he stays out of it. He doesn't want to get involved with them and their problems."

So the stepfather in that house evolved as a shadowy kind of parental figure. Not wishing to walk a tightrope in matters of family discord this parent bowed out of the discipline picture.

If a real father is around, stepfathers will often view this as an additional reason for avoiding any discipline of stepchildren. If the other parent is also remarried and all the parents, with their differing ideas, were to feel entitled to reprimand the child, he might feel confused about the varying demands made upon him.

A constructive stepfather who develops a sense of responsibility toward his wife's children may feel that he has a right to exact certain behavior from them. If the wife is not resentful of such a position, the results can be helpful and offer guidance for the children. But more often, stepparents have to stifle their true feelings. These reactions may run the gamut from wanting to interfere to a hope that their stepkids will disappear and stop causing so much trouble. There are bound to be frustrations on both sides of the discipline fence.

Other dilemmas may occur in a family where the two remarried parents have new children who are being raised with *his* or *her* children. Both parents will discipline *their* children, but often only one will rebuke *his* or *her* kids.

If discipline includes physical punishment, a child may be very resentful of a spanking given him by a stepfather. There may always be the suspicion that a real parent would have reacted otherwise toward the child.

There are many kinds of irritating behavior that a parent will accept from his own child that he will find objectionable in a stepchild. When a parent remarries, for instance, and a stepchild transfers his anger at something else and takes it out on the new stepmother or stepfather, it requires tact and diplomacy to be understanding without seeming to ignore the situation. This new parent must listen to the child and try to understand the child's hurt without permitting himself to be used as a punching bag.

There are many times when it is difficult to say *no* to a stepchild. It is often much easier to retreat if a child is testing an adult. When a child is unduly resentful of a stepparent's position, discipline is probably best left to the devices of the real parent. The stepparent should dispense with any disciplinary action until the relationship has improved and is on a sure footing.

## Conclusion

Bad as divorce is for children, many authorities now feel that children are probably better off in a happy single-parent home than they would be in a discordant, strife-torn home with both parents. There is not much stability for a child raised in such a chaotic environment.

Divorce has to be a stressful period for everyone involved. But the trauma of divorce to children can be lessened by large doses of parental love and emotional support urging acceptance and understanding of new living arrangements. Where these new conditions perplex, the parent must try to aid the child by suggesting constructive attitudes over and over and over again.

So often it seems that if the courts did not make it mandatory for parents to make some provisions for the children of divorce, a much higher number would be left to the care of our social institutions. As is, many children live out much of their lives in contact with only one parent.

For the parents and children who remain involved with each other, they must learn the importance of compromise. The child must do what is best for himself without destroying the parents' right to enjoy their lives too. Parents cannot forever forfeit their own desires for the sake of the children, yet most often the needs of the child must be considered before those of the adult.

How much compromise is too much and how much is not enough? The answers lie with each individual. The way in which one learns to handle any situation relates to his knowledge of the art of living.

Many of the problems of childhood occur to children of wedded parents as well as to children of divorce, but the destruction of a child's security by parental separation makes him much more vulnerable to unhappiness. Awareness of the child's frailty is the first step toward successful handling of his fears that he, too, was divorced along with his parents.

# Part IV

# SUGGESTED READING and OTHER HELPFUL INFORMATION

# RELATED READING

The following lists some of the more recent books that may be of further help for divorced parents.

*A Smart Kid Like You* by Stella Pevsner. The Seabury Press, New York, 1975.
Nina, a seventh grader, finds that her new math teacher is dad's new wife. Excellent fiction.

*Are Parents Bad for Children* by Graham B. Blaine, Jr., Coward, McCann and Geoghegan Inc., New York, 1973.
Parents in relationship to their alienated children and some suggestions for a different way of life.

*The Boys and Girls Book About Divorce* by Richard A. Gardner, Bantam Books, Inc., New York, 1970.
Very good book that explains the personal problems of divorce to children from about fifth grade and up.

*Children of Separation and Divorce* edited by Irving R. Stuart and Lawrence E. Abt, Grossman Publishers, New York, 1972.
Sections written by different people all offering their views for dealing with problems relating to children of the divorced.

*Creative Divorce* by Mel Krantzler, New American Library, New York, 1973.
A positive approach to accepting divorce and rebuilding a new life.

*Divorced in America* by Joseph Epstein, E.P. Dutton and Co., New York, 1974.
Recounting one man's divorce in which mom leaves and dad raises the children. Very good.

*Divorce* by Lionel Felder, World Publishing Co., New York and Cleveland, 1971.
The divorce process from first consideration through the settlement.

*Financial Guideline: Divorce* by Arthur Cuse, Guideline Publishing Co., Los Angeles, 1971.
Detailing the financial side of divorce from attorneys' fees to pre-nuptial agreements when you remarry.

*Getting It Together* by Lynn Forman, Berkley Publishing Corp., New York, 1974.
Breezy account of how to get along as a single parent.

*The Half-Parent* by Brenda Maddox, M. Evans and Co., Inc., New York, 1975.
How to parent someone else's children. Good.

*Inside Divorce:* Is It What You Really Want? by Edmond Addeo and Robert Burger. Chilton Book Co., Radnor, Pennsylvania, 1975.
Surveys divorced people in a guide for looking before you plunge.

*Mama Doesn't Live Here Anymore* by Judy Sullivan, Arthur Field's Books, Inc., New York, 1974.
Mama leaves child, husband and the midwest to find herself in the woman's movement.

*Marital Separation* by Robert S. Weiss, Basic Books, Inc., New York, 1975.
Suggestions for those who are or will be separated.

*No-Fault Divorce* by Michael Wheeler, Beacon Press, Boston, 1974.
Discusses need for divorce to be achieved without finding one or both parties at fault.

*Separation Journal of a Marriage* by Eve Baguedor, Simon and Schuester, New York, 1972.
The emotional wrench of separation and the painful growth of self reliance.

*The Single Parent Experience* by Carol Klein, Avon Books, New York, 1973.
Child-raising by an unmarried parent.

*Stepchild in the Family* by Anne W. Simon, Odessey Press, New York, 1964.
Explaining the problems of stepchildren and their stepparents at a time when both are on the increase.

*Uncoupling* by Norman Sheresky and Marya Mannes, The Viking Press, New York, 1972.
The law and emotional realism when a marriage is coming apart.

*Where is Daddy?* by Beth Goff, Beacon Press, Boston, 1969.
Fictional story that brings the situation of divorce down to young children's level of understanding.

*Women in Transition* (A Feminist Handbook on Separation and Divorce), Charles Scribner's Sons, New York, 1975.
Divorce information accented by personal experiences.

# HELPFUL AGENCIES *

Most of the organizations listed are not-for-profit agencies which can be contacted for more detailed information.

## Key
**Fr.** Free. Counseling available without payment.
**M.F.** Modest fee required.
**S.F.S.** Sliding fee scale. Pay according to ability.
**G.** Works with groups.
**G.F.** Family groups only.
**I.** Individual counseling.
**D.** Do not counsel but will direct persons seeking help to the proper agency. Often have information about many other agencies.
**S.G.** Offers help through support groups.
**S.H.** Self-help groups.

## ALASKA

Department of Health and Social Services
Division of Social Services
Pouch H-05
Juneau, Alaska 99811
**I, G, Fr.**

## ARIZONA

Arizona Department of Economic Security
1717 Jefferson
Phoenix, Arizona 85005
P.O. Box 6123
**G.F. Fr. (If eligible)**

## CALIFORNIA

Catholic Big Brothers, Inc.
.1800 N. Highland, Suite 412
Los Angeles, California 90028
464-8257
**I, G, Fr.**

---

\* The author does not endorse any of the listed organizations but suggests them for the further investigation of the reader.

# DADDY DOESN'T LIVE HERE ANYMORE

Center for Women's Studies and Services
908 'F' Street
San Diego, California 92101
714-233-8984
**I, G, Fr.**

Childcare Switchboard
3896 24th Street
San Francisco, California 94114
282-7858
**I, G.**

Oakland Feminist Women's Health Center
Women's Choice Clinic
2930 McClure
Oakland, California 94609
**I, G, S.F.S.**

Big Sisters and Big Sister's Home
Big Sisters League Inc.
115 Redwood Street
San Diego, California 92103
714-297-1172
Big Sisters — **Fr.**
Big Sister's Temporary home - **Set Fee M.F.**

Children's Home Society of California
3100 W. Adams Blvd.
Los Angeles, California 90018
735-1351
**I, G, S.F.S.**

Divorce Services of America
704 Santa Monica Blvd.
Santa Monica, California 90040
800-421-7239 (Toll free)
**Helps people obtain inexpensive divorce**

Info
Information and Referral Service of
L.A. County, Inc.
621 South Virgil Ave.
Los Angeles, California 90005
**D.**

United Way
Western Region
11646 W. Pico Blvd.
Los Angeles, California 90064
213-879-0910
**D**

University of California Extension
Women's Opportunity Center
Irvine, California 92717
**G (For members)**

We Care
121 Broadway
#517
San Diego, California 92101
**S.H.**

## COLORADO

Dept. of Social Services
1575 Sherman St.
Denver, Colorado 80203
**D, I, S.F.S.**

Women Enterprises
158 Fillmore
#307
Denver, Colorado 80220
**I, G. (inquire about fees)**

## CONNECTICUT

The Center for the Person in Transition
26 Trumbull Street
New Haven, Connecticut 06511
562-9872
**I, G, S.F.S.**

Information and Counseling Service for Women
301 Crown Street
New Haven, Connecticut
**I, G, M.F.**

Counseling Collective
Women's Center
U-118 U. Conn.
Storrs, Connecticut 06268
I, Free

## DELAWARE

Family Services of Northern Delaware
809 Washington St.
Wilmington, Delaware 19801
302-654-5303
I, G, Fr., S.F.S.

## FLORIDA

Dept. of Health and Rehabilitative Services
Social and Economic Services Program Office
1323 Winewood Blvd.
Tallahassee, Florida 32301
D.

Florida State University Women's Center
University Box 6826
110 N. Woodward Ave.
Tallahassee, Florida 32313
904-644-4007
I, G, D, S.F.S.

Jacksonville Women's Movement, Inc.
P.O. Box 10551
Jacksonville, Florida 32207
Feminist Counseling
Fr., or M.F.

## HAWAII

State of Hawaii
Department of Social Services and Housing
P.O. Box 339
Honolulu, Hawaii 96809
I, G, Fr., (If eligible)

## IOWA

Beloit of Iowa
A Children's Service Center of the
American Lutheran Church
1323 Northwestern
Ames, Iowa 50010
515-232-7262
**I, G.**

Y.M.C.A.
Alumni Hall
Iowa State University
Ames, Iowa 50011
**D.**

Open Line, Inc.
2502 Knapp
Ames, Iowa 50010
**I, D, Fr.**

State of Iowa
Department of Social Services
3619½ Douglas Ave.
Des Moines, Iowa 50310
**I, G, D, Fr.**

Youth and Shelter Services, Inc.
804 Kellogg Ave.
Ames, Iowa 50010
515-233-3141
**I, G, Fr., or S.F.S.**

## ILLINOIS

Americas Society of Divorced Men
575 Keep St.
Elgin, Illinois 60120
312-695-2200
**For members only - Dues**

Divorce Adjustment Institute
708 Church St.
Evanston, Illinois 60201
312-864-2100
**Conducts seminars - S.F.**

Divorce Anonymous
P.O. Box 5313
Chicago, Illinois 60680
S.H.

Evanston Hospital
Crises Intervention/ Referral Service
2650 Ridge Ave.
Evanston, Illinois 60201
312-492-2000
I, S.F.S.

Family Service Bureau
United Charities of Chicago
64 East Jackson Blvd.
Chicago, Illinois 60604
312-939-1300
I, G, S.F.S.

Family Service of Winnetka-Northfield
992½ Linden Ave.
Winnetka, Illinois 60093
312-446-8060
I, G.

Jewish Family and Community Service
One South Franklin St.
Chicago, Illinois 60606
I. G, S.F.S.

Northwest Mental Health Center
1616 N. Arlington Heights Road
Arlington Heights, Illinois 60004
312-392-1420
(A not-for-profit organization)
I, G, S.F.S.

Northshore Mental Health Association and
Irene Josselyn Clinic
405 Central Ave.
Northfield, Illinois 60093
I, G, S.F.S.

Orchard Center for Mental Health
8600 Gross Point Road
Skokie, Illinois 60076
312-967-7300
**I, G, S.F.S.**

Our Children's Foundation
Daley Civic Center
Dearborn and Washington
Chicago, Illinois 60611
312-443-6252 or 312-443-6394
Day Care Center available to children while parents are in litigation in the courtrooms. Must be referred by judge or attorney.

Parental Stress Services
P.O. Box 809
Evanston, Illinois 60204
312-463-0390
**G.**

South Suburban Y.W.C.A.
45 Plaza
Park Forest, Illinois 60466
312-748-5660
**G, M.F.**

Young Women's Christian Association
of Metropolitan Chicago
Loop Center
37 S. Wabash Ave.
Chicago, Illinois 60603
**I, Fr., or S.F.S.**

# KANSAS

State Dept. of Social and Rehabilitation
Services
State Office Building
Topeka, Kansas 66612
**D.**

## KENTUCKY

Department for Human Resources
Bureau for Social Services
403 Wapping St.
Frankfort, Kentucky 40601
Basic Counseling
**Fr. (To citizens of Kentucky)**

## MAINE

State of Maine
Department of Human Services
Augusta, Maine 04333
**G.F., Fr.**

## MASSACHUSETTS

Everywoman's Center
Goodell Hall
University of Massachusetts
Amherst, Massachusetts 01002
**I, G, Fr. or M.F.**

The Women's Counseling and
Resources Center, Inc.
1555 Massachusetts Ave.
Cambridge, Mass. 02192
**I, S.F.S.**

## MICHIGAN

Department Social Services
300 S. Capitol Ave.
Lansing, Michigan 48926
**I, D, Fr. (If eligible)**

## MINNESOTA

University of Minnesota
Minnesota Women's Center
301 Walter Library
Minneapolis, Minnesota 55455
612-373-3850
**G, D.**

## NEBRASKA

Department of Public Welfare
301 Centennial Mall South
5th Floor
Lincoln, Nebraska 68509
**D.**

## NEW HAMPSHIRE

New Dynamics Associates
Box 92 R.F.D. #5
Laconia, New Hampshire 03246
603-524-1441
Courses
**G (or couples), M.F.**

## NEW JERSEY

EVE
Kean College of New Jersey
Morris Ave.
Union, New Jersey 07083
**Workshops whenever scheduled**

Y.W.C.A. of Essex and West Hudson
395 Main Street
Orange, New Jersey 07050
201-672-9500
**I, G, M.F.**

## NEW MEXICO

State of New Mexico
Health and Social Services Department
P.O. Box 2348
Santa Fe, New Mexico 87503
**G, I, Fr.(If eligible)**

The University of New Mexico
Women's Center
1824 Las Lomas N.E.
Albuquerque, New Mexico 87106
505-277-3716
**G, D, Fr.**

## NEW YORK

Department of Social Services
40 North Pearl Street
Albany, New York 12243
D.

Family Service Association of America
44 East 23rd Street
New York, New York 10010
212-674-6100
D (Will refer to 300 agencies in 42 states and 6 Canadian provinces), S.F.S.

National Association for Divorced Women, Inc.
Pan Am Bldg.
200 Park Ave.
Suite 303 East
New York, New York 10017
212-344-8407

## NORTH CAROLINA

County of Durham
Community Mental Health Center
414 East Main Street
Durham, North Carolina 27701
I, G, Fr., M.F.

Durham Women's Center Y.W.C.A.
312 Umstead Street
Durham, North Carolina 27707
919-688-4396
S.G., M.F.

State of North Carolina
Department of Human Resources
Division of Social Services
325 N. Salisbury Street
Raleigh, North Carolina 27611
I, G. (Fees set by agency standards)

## NORTH DAKOTA

Director Community Services Division
Social Service Board of North Dakota
15th Floor, State Capitol Bldg.
Bismarck, North Dakota 58505
**I, G, Fr. or S.F.S.**

## OHIO

Cleveland Women's Counsel
P.O. Box 18472
Cleveland Heights, Ohio 44118
**S.G.**

## OKLAHOMA

State of Oklahoma
Oklahoma Public Welfare Commission
Department of Institutions, Social and Rehabilitative Services
Box #25352
Oklahoma City, Oklahoma 73125
**D**

## PENNSYLVANIA

Big Brothers/Big Sisters of America
220 Suburban Station Building
Philadelphia, Pennsylvania 19103
**I, G; also a supervised one-to-one
program of friendship between an adult
and a matched child from a single-parent
home. 357 affiliates.**

Commonwealth of Pennsylvania
Department of Public Welfare
P.O. Box 2675
Harrisburg, Pennsylvania 17120
**D.**

## SOUTH CAROLINA

South Carolina Department of Social Services
P.O. Box 1520
Columbia, South Carolina 29202
**I, G, F, D.**

## SOUTH DAKOTA

Department of Social Services
Division of Human Development
Office of Community Services
State Office Bldg.
Illinois Street
Pierre, South Dakota 57501
605-224-3227
**I, G, D, S.F.S.**

## UTAH

State of Utah
Division of Family Services
333 South 2nd East
Salt Lake City, Utah 84111
**I, G, S.F.S.**

## VERMONT

State of Vermont
Department of Social and Rehabilitation Services
Agency of Human Services
81 River Street
Montpelier, Vermont 05602
**I, D, Fr.**

## VIRGINIA

Family and Children's Services of Richmond
1518 Willow Lawn Drive
Richmond, Virginia 23230
**Fr. or S.F.S.**

## WASHINGTON

State of Washington
Department of Social and Health Services
Olympia, Wahington 98504
**I, G, Fr.**

Seattle Counseling Center
1505 Broadway
Seattle, Washington 98122
206-329-8707
**I, G, S.F.S.**

Women's Divorce Cooperative
University Y.W.C.A.
4224 University Way N.E.
Seattle, Washington 98105
**Workshops, S.F.S.**

## WASHINGTON D.C.

Action
Foster Grandparents Program
Washington, D.C. 20525
800-424-8580 (Toll free)

## WISCONSIN

Division of Community Services
1 W. Wilson Street
Madison, Wisconsin 53702
**D.**

Women's Crises Line, Inc.
2211 E. Kenwood Blvd.
Milwaukee, Wisconsin 53211
964-7535
**I, Fr. or S.F.S.**

## OREGON

Children's Services Division
Public Service Building
Salem, Oregon 97310
**I, G, Fr.**

# BIBLIOGRAPHY

Abrams, Maxine. "Sibling Numerology: How Birth Order Affects Behavior," Town and Country Magazine, October 1976.

Albrecht, Margaret. *A Complete Guide for the Working Mother*. New York: Award Books, 1967.

Anthony, E.J., and Koupernick, C., editors. *Family: Children As a Psychiatric Risk*. Vol. 3. Wiley and Sons, Inc., 1974.

Baguedor, Eve. *Separation Journal of a Marriage*. New York: Simon and Schuster, 1972.

Benjamin, James. *Divorce: For Better or for Worse*. ABC Television Network Program, Broadcast Thursday, December 16, 1976, 10:00 - 11:00 PM, EST.

Bernard, Jessie. *The Future of Marriage*. New York: Bantam Books, 1972: pp. 19, 134, 190-198.

Bledsoe, Eugene. "Teaching About Divorce," *National Education Association*, January-February, 1977: p. 31.

Bowlby, John. *Child Care and the Growth of Love*. Baltimore, Maryland: Penguin Books, 1965.

"Boys in Fatherless Homes," U.S. Department of Health, Education and Welfare. Office of Child Development. Children's Bureau, 1971.

Braun, Charlotte. "Separate But Equal Parenting," *Chicago Tribune*. Lifestyle, December 5, 1976.

Brooker, Betsy. "Focus — The Children of Divorce," *Chicago Daily News*, April 27, 1977.

Callahan, Sidney Cornelia. *Parenting Principles and Politics of Parenthood*. Baltimore, Maryland: Penguin Books, Inc., 1974.

Cattell, Psyche, Ed. D. *Raising Children With Love and Limits*. Chicago, Nelson-Hall Company, 1972: p. 158.

Chess, Stella: *An Introduction to Child Psychiatry*. New York: Grune and Stratton, 1959: pp. 170-177.

Cuse, Arthur. *Financial Guidelines: Divorce*. Los Angeles: Guideline Publishing Co., 1971: p. 140.

Dusky, Lorraine. "A Natural Mother Speaks Out On Adoptees' Right to Know," Town and Country Magazine, October, 1976.

Despert, J. Louise, *Children of Divorce*. New York: Doubleday and Co., Inc., 1953: pp. 66-67, 116-150.

"Divorce", *MD Medical Magazine*, Vol. 21, No. 3, March 1977.

Dodson, Fitzhugh. *How to Father.* New York: New American Library, 1974.

"Do Working Wives Risk Divorce?" Right Now, *McCalls Magazine,* September, 1976: p. 41.

Dreikers, Rudolph M.D. with Vicki Soltz, R.N. *Children: The Challenge.* New York: Duell, Sloan and Pearce, 1964: pp. 145, 172.

Ephron, Delia. "The State of the Union," *Esquire Magazine,* February, 1977.

Erikson, Erik H. *Insight and Responsibility.* New York: W.W. Norton and Co., 1964: pp. 83-107.

Epstein, Joseph. *Divorced In America.* New York: Penguin Books, Inc., 1974: pp. 175-202.

Felder, Raoul Lionel. *Divorce.* New York: World Publishing Co., 1971.

Flaste, Richard. *"You and Your Child,"* Chicago Tribune. January 17, 1977.

Friggens, Paul. "If You Spoil The Marriage, Spare The Child," Readers Digest, June, 1975.

Forman, Lynn. *Getting It Together.* New York: Berkley Publishing Corporation, 1974: pp. 43, 86.

Fredelle. "The New Single Woman," *Woman's Day.* April 5, 1977: p. 34.

Fromm, Eric. *The Art of Loving.* New York: Harper and Row Publishers, 1956: pp. 38-52, 59.

Gardner, Richard A. *The Boys and Girls Book About Divorce.* New York: Bantam Books, Inc., 1970.

Gardner, Richard A. *Psychotherapy With Children of Divorce.* New York: Jason Aronson, Inc., 1976.

Gettleman, Susan and Janet Markowitz. *The Courage to Divorce.* New York: Simon and Schuster, 1974.

Gilbert, Sara D. *What's A Father For.* New York: Warner Books, 1975: pp. 193-195, 203.

Ginott, Haim G. *Between Parent and Child.* New York: Avon Books, 1965.

Goode, William J. *The Family.* Englewood, Cliffs, New Jersey: Prentice-Hall, Inc., 1964.

Goodman, Ellen. "Is Love Better The Seventh Time Around?" *Sunday Sun-Times.* December 12, 1976.

Greene, Bernard L. *A Clinical Approach to Marital Problems.* Springfield, Illinois: Charles C. Thomas, 1970: p. 193.

Goodman, David *What's Best For Your Child and You.* New

York: National Board of Young Men's Christian Association Press, 1966.

Greer, Germaine, *The Female Eunuch.* New York: McGraw-Hill Book Co., 1971.

Grollman, Earl A. *Explaining Divorce to Children.* Boston: Beacon Press, 1969.

Harris, Thomas A. *I'm O.K. - You're O.K.* New York: Avon Books, 1969: pp. 228-245.

Haussman, Florence and Mary Ann Guitar. *Divorce Handbook.* New York: G.P. Putnam's Sons, 1960.

Hirsch, Barbara B. *What A Woman Needs to Know.* New York: Bantam Books, Inc., 1973: pp. 105-111.

Hope, Karol and Nancy Young, Editors. *Momma: The Sourcebook for Single Mothers.* New York: New American Library, 1976: pp. 166-171, 206-281.

Hunt, Morton M. *The World Of The Formerly Married.* New York: McGraw-Hill Book Co., 1966: pp. 50, 261.

Huxley, Julian. *Man In The Modern World.* New York: New American Library of World Literature, Inc., 1955.

Ilg, Frances L. and Louise Bates Ames, *Child Behavior.* New York: Harper and Row, 1955.

Iversen, William. "No-Fault Parenthood: All It Takes Is Love and Honesty," *Town and Country Mazazine.* October, 1976.

Jones, Eve. *Raising Your Child in a Fatherless Home.* New-York: Free Press of Glencoe, 1963.

Joseph, Harry and Gordon Zern. *The Emotional Problems Of Children.* New York: Crown Publishers, Inc., 1954.

King, Barbara. "Children of Divorce: How To Help Them When The Split Comes," *Town and Country Magazine.* October, 1976.

Krantzler, Mel. *Creative Divorce.* New York: New American Library, 1973: pp. 205-240.

Klein, Carole. *The Single Parent Experience.* New York: Avon Books, 1973: pp. 253-259.

Lake, Alice. "Divorcees: The New Poor," *McCalls Magazine,* September, 1976; p. 18.

LeShan, Eda. "When Mother Love Goes Too Far," *Woman's Day,* April 5, 1977: p. 150.

Lorenz, Konrad. *On Aggression.* New York: Bantam Books, 1966.

Lynn, David B. *The Father.* Monterey, California: Brooks/Cole Publishing Co., 1974: pp. 10-11.

Maddox, Brenda. *The Half-Parent.* New York: M. Evans and Co., Inc., 1975.

Maier, Henry D. *Three Theories of Child Development.* New York: Harper and Row, Publishers, 1965: pp. 241-280.

May, Rollo. *Love and Will.* New York: W.W. Norton and Co., Inc., 1969.

McGrady, Patrick. "A Lifestyle To Avoid Aging," *Woman's Day.* April 5, 1977: p. 81.

Montagu, Ashley M.F., Ed. *Man and Agression.* New York: Oxford University Press, 1968.

Montague, Louise. "Straight Talk About The Living-Together Arrangement,"*Readers Digest* April, 1977: p. 91.

Menninger, Karl. *Love Against Hate.* New York: Harcourt, Brace and Co., 1942: pp. 7-40.

Menninger, William C. and Munro Leaf. *You and Psychiatry.* New York: Charles Scribner's Sons, 1948: pp. 139-152.

Morgan, Elaine. *The Descent of Woman.* New York: Stein and Day, 1972.

Morris, Desmond. *The Human Zoo.* New York: McGraw-Hill Book Co., 1969.

Morris, Desmond, *The Naked Ape.* New York: Dell Publishing Co., Inc., 1967.

Murphy, Gardner. *Psychological Thought from Pythagoras to Freud.* New York: Harcourt, Brace and World Inc., 1968.

Nauton, Edna. "Divorce - Is It The Easy Way Out?" *Miami Herald* Thursday, February 10, 1977.

Neubauer, Peter, Editor. *The Process of Child Development.* New York: New American Library, 1976.

"One Parent Families," U.S. Department of Health, Education and Welfare. Office of Human Development Children's Bureau, 1974.

Parkhurst, Helen C. *Exploring the Child's World.* New York: Appleton-Century Crofts, Inc., 1951.

Pascoe, Elizabeth Jean. "Helping Children Survive Divorce." *Woman's Day,* August, 1976.

Pevsner, Stella. *A Smart Kid Like You.* New York: The Seabury Press, 1975.

Porter, Sylvia. "Social Security System Robs Women of Benefits," *Chicago Sun-Times,* Wednesday, February 9, 1977.

Pringle, Mia Kellmer. *The Needs of Children.* New York: Schocken Books, 1975: p. 128.

Quinn, Jane Bryant. "Money Facts," *Woman's Day*, April 5, 1977: p. 30.

Redondo, Diego and Edith Freund. *Growing Up Healthy*. Matteson, Illinois: Greatlakes Living Press, 1976: p. 60.

Reich, Charles A. *The Greening of America* New York: Random House, 1970.

Roll, Sue Lindsay. "Getting Along With Your Ex," *Chicago Sun-Times*. Sunday, October 17, 1976.

Rubin, Theodore I. "Psychiatrists Notebook," *Ladies Home Journal*. November, 1976: p. 62.

Sandstrom, C.I. *The Psychology of Childhood and Adolesence*. Baltimore, Maryland: Penguin Books, Inc., 1966: pp. 140-184.

Schwarz, Berthold Eric and Bartholomew A. Ruggieri. *Parent-Child Tensions*. Philadelphia: J.B. Lippincott Co., 1958: pp. 85-105, 205-217.

Sheresky, Norman and Marya Mannes. *Uncoupling: The Art of Coming Apart*. New York: Viking Press, 1972: p. 125.

Simon, Anne W. *Step Child In The Family*. New York: The Odessey Press, 1964.

Spock, Dr. Benjamin. *Baby and Child Care*. New York: Pantheon Books, 1969: pp. 190-194.

Steinzor, Bernard. *When Parents Divorce*. New York: Pantheon Books, 1969: pp. 190-194.

Streshinsky, Shirley. "How Divorce Really Affects Children," *Redbook Magazine*. September, 1976.

Stuart, Irving R. and Lawrence E. Abt, Editors. *Children of Separation and Divorce*. New York: Grossman Publishers, 1972.

Talbot, Nathan B. *Raising Children in Modern America*. Boston: Little Brown and Co., 1974.

Toffler, Alvin. *Future Shock*. New York: Random House, 1970.

*News and World Report*. "Who Stays Married Longer." U.S. News and World Report. October 30, 1972.

"The Vulnerable Child," U.S. Department of Health, Education and Welfare. Office of Child Development Services, 1970.

Wahlroos, Sven. *Family Communications*. New York: New American Library, 1974: pp. 293-296

Wallerstein, Judith S. and Joan B. Kelly. "The Effects of Parental Divorce: The Adolescent Experience,"

Wallerstein, Judith and Joan B. Kelly. "The Effects of Parental Divorce: Experience of the Preschool Child," *Journal of the Academy of Child Psychiatry.* New Haven, Yale University Press. Vol. 14, No. 4, Autumn, 1975.

Watzlawick, Paul and Janet Helmick Beavin and Don D. Jackson. *Pragmatics of Human Communication.* New York: W.W. Norton and Co., Inc., 1967.

"We the Youth of America." U.S. Public Information Office, Bureau of the Census, June, 1973.

Weiss, Robert S. *Marital Separation.* New York: Basic Books, Inc., 1975.

*Women and Poverty.* Staff Report. United States Commission on Civil Rights, June, 1974.

*Women in Transition: A Feminist Handbook on Separation and Divorce.* New York: Charles Scribners Sons, 1975.

Ziman, Edmund. *Jealousy in Children.* New York: A.A. Wyn, Inc., 1949.